Eight Months in Provence

A Junior Year Abroad 30 Years Late

Eight Months in Provence
A Junior Year Abroad 30 Years Late

Marshall & McClintic Publishing
200 Coyote Street #1122, Nevada City, CA 95959
MarshallMcClinticPublishing.com

Diane Covington-Carter's back cover photo
by Kial James, Nevada City, CA

This book is set in Adobe® Garamond Type Text.
Printed in the United States of America
First Edition: June 2016

ISBN-13: 978-0-9910446-3-4
ISBN-10: 0991044630

To my two French "sisters"
Huguette DesClos and Maïté LeDantec,
for your love and friendship, in French

Table of Contents

For time may excite us or divert us…
but when we look back,
the only things we cherish are those
which in some way met our original want;
the desire which formed in us in early youth,
undirected and of its own accord.

Willa Cather, *Song of the Lark*

Prologue

May, 1999, Aix-en-Provence, France

I wandered through the winding cobblestone streets of the *vielle ville,* the old town, of Aix-en-Provence, thrilled to be visiting a place that had jumped out of guide books at me for years, reaching for my attention. The ancient town, in the south of France, was founded by the Romans because of its *source,* or spring, and over fifty fountains flowed, bubbled and splashed on different corners of the village.

For two days I followed the maze-like streets, delightfully lost. When I'd find myself back at *la Place de la Mairie,* the central plaza of the old town, it felt like arriving in the center of a labyrinth. I'd recognize the large fountain and the thir-teenth-century clock tower and experience a sense of calm. Ah yes, here I am again.

On my last evening in Aix, the soft glow of twilight reflect-ed off the tall French doors and windows of the seventeenth century buildings around the plaza, with their black wrought iron balconies and white shutters. The merry splashing of the fountain mixed with the chatter of French and the laughter of children as they chased each other nearby. The clock tower bells rang out the hour, as they had for over seven centuries. Eight o'clock.

How wondrous to be in a place that had not changed for hundreds of years. If these cobblestones could talk, oh the tales they could tell.

I sat down at an outdoor café and ordered a glass of rosé wine, a specialty of the region. A soft spring breeze rustled the new spring leaves on the giant plane trees around the plaza.

As I sipped the light, chilled wine, a deep sense of contentment washed over me. The words of American writer Willa Cather, in her essay from her travels in France in the early 20th century came to mind.

One cannot divine or forecast the conditions that will make happiness; one only stumbles upon them by chance, in a lucky hour, at the world's end somewhere, and holds fast to the days, as to fortune or fame.

I wanted to hold fast to these past two days and the sense of my own 'lucky hour.'

This is where I'll stay when I come to live in France, I thought. It feels right. I can trust that.

1

You have to be friendly with the uncertainty in yourself.
Louis B. Jones, author

La Rêve: The Dream
Fall 1999

"I'm going to France for eight months, to do my 'junior year abroad, thirty years late,'" I'd say to people as I prepared for my trip. It surprised me how many greeted my statement with wonder, excitement, even glee. One woman gasped, took my hand and looked into my eyes.

"Please know that you're doing this for all women," she said.

Others however, were not so encouraging. One relative had these harsh words to say.

"What do you think you are doing, going off for eight months like that?"

I listened, caught my breath and then spoke up to her.

"What dreams have you let die that you have to criticize me for wanting to fulfill mine?" She had no answer to that and seemed as stunned as I was from my response. I felt proud of myself for being that bold, not my normal behavior in my family.

But she had hit on a tender spot and her words would not have upset me unless I also harbored doubts myself. It was true that my life was not perfect and possibly the time was not the best to leave for eight months. But in thirty years of waiting to fulfill this desire to live in France, I'd discovered that there never *was* a perfect time.

I was fifty years old. Did I even have another thirty years left?

I remembered words that a therapist and teacher had quoted to me years before.

"If I am not for myself, then who can I be for? And if not now, when?"

If not now, when? I mentally went over the pros and cons of my journey, for the hundredth time.

My beloved sister had been fighting brain tumors for five years. I shuddered to think of what lay ahead in that journey. But at this moment, after two surgeries, chemo and radiation, she seemed stable. That gave me a window.

I'd been promoting a personal growth seminar for three and a half years that had wound down. I was supposed to receive some residual income from people who were continuing with ongoing coaching. The completion of that project provided a gap in which I could take this time in France to focus on writing, which was my passion and always ended up getting pushed to a back burner in my busy life.

I could rent out my home and cover the mortgage and live more cheaply in a small apartment in France.

Royce, my supportive boyfriend, understood how much I wanted to go. I'd told him from the beginning, a year before, that I had to go in search of the nineteen-year-old young woman who hadn't gone to live in France all those years before. He was even driving me to the airport.

My daughters were grown up and living their own busy lives.

Now, the drawbacks of going. Thirty years before, I didn't

go because I was having a baby. Now, my daughter was having my first grandbaby, three months before I was planning to leave. Would I be a terrible grandmother to leave for eight months? When I shared my doubts with them, my son-in-law took me aside.

"You have your whole life to be a grandma. You should go."

He helped me to see that I was about to put off my wish one more time. How many times did I have left to do that? We made plans that they would come and visit with the baby at the end of my stay.

My financial situation, which had never been my strong suit, posed another challenge. Even with the potential residual income and reduced expenses, would I be able to generate additional revenue during those eight months?

Two and a half years before, I'd bought a run-down eight-acre organic apple farm. It had belonged to my elderly neighbors, who had planted each tree and tended the place with love for fifty years. I had no business buying it on my own, but couldn't stand that a developer was lined up to purchase it.

Since then, I'd spent all my resources–time, energy and money–on the farm, clearing, pruning, harvesting, and selling apples. Then I worked on the house, cleaning, painting, plastering, tearing up old green linoleum and refinishing vintage pine floors till the old place shone. The farm represented my 'nest egg.' My bank account, didn't reflect a lot of spare cash.

An astrologer had told me once that I had never been on a career path, but rather on a vision quest. That was true. My whole adult life I'd chosen ways to generate income based on flexibility to work around my daughters' schedules and on whether or not the work pointed towards freedom, for myself and others.

I had sold time management systems, promoted business and personal growth seminars, learned to be a life coach, been a free-lance writer and taught writing classes, among other hats

I'd worn. Surely, in France, I would be able to use some of my varied skills to bring in additional cash to sustain myself, as I always had?

And lastly, was I crazy to take a leap of faith into the unknown, to a town I'd only visited for two whole days, where I knew no one?

There were no guarantees and underneath the excitement of preparing to leave I wasn't as sure of myself as I wanted to be. I wanted to trust, but had an inner harsh voice that talked to me in my head.

"You are fifty years old. You should have more to show for your life by now and more financial stability. Who do you think you are gallivanting off to France for eight months? When are you going to be responsible? Don't you know that normal people give up on their dreams? When are you going to be normal?"

That voice sounded remarkably like my mother's and those words stung deep into shame that I had carried for as long as I could remember, shame that I was somehow not enough.

And yet, France, and the memory of my time in Aix-en-Provence, the plaza with the fountain and the old clock tower lived inside of me, a precious place where I had experienced those moments of pure happiness, a sense of my own 'lucky hour.' And ever since I began studying French at age fourteen, I'd experienced a thrilling aliveness when I spoke the soft, musical, sounds of the language.

Joseph Campbell said, "Follow your bliss." Could I do that? I had to trust and believe, in myself, in my longings and in life.

The plan was set into motion now. It was too late to turn back. I, along with my fifty years of imperfect history, was going to live in France.

I was going to "follow my bliss."

2

*Uncover what you long for
and you will discover who you are.*

Phil Cousineau,
The Art of Pilgrimage: The Seeker's Guide to Making Travel Sacred

Le Départ: The Departure
November 3, 1999

The big jet, partially empty, had rolled back from the gate, taxied into position and waited for the signal to speed down the runway. It must have been a routine Wednesday for the flight crew, on this San Francisco to Paris flight, with everyone buckled in and quiet.

But for me, it was anything *but* a routine Wednesday. I sat still in my seat, going over the past months, weeks and finally days and hours that had led up to that moment.

I'd packed up all the personal things in my home, photos and other treasured pieces of my past. The handmade pottery person my daughter Heather made me when she was ten got lowered into a box of its own, surrounded with tissue paper. I noted how one of his skinny legs had been carefully glued back onto his round body. I tucked a few photos of my family into my suitcase.

I'd found trustworthy renters for my house, a huge piece of the puzzle that fell into place just a week before my departure date.

I'd said goodbye to my two daughters and my new grand-baby Ellie, who would change so much while I was gone. My sister Sharon, with her vicious brain tumors, supported me in going and hoped to come and visit. Royce dropped me off at the airport with a beautiful card wishing me to have 'the time of my life' while I lived out this long held desire.

I held each of them tight, sensing their preciousness in my life.

My one small rolling bag was checked into the hull of the airplane, as few clothes as I could possibly pack because, who, after all, would take clothes to France. As my mother would say, that would be like "taking coals to Newcastle."

The jet engines revved and startled me back from my thoughts. We began to roll, picking up speed, then lifted into the air. Out the window, the Golden Gate Bridge stood out-lined against the sparkling blue water of the San Francisco Bay. So beautiful.

For a moment, I felt a stab of fear in my stomach. What had I done, leaving everything and everyone behind? My home, my friends, my family, and a perfectly good life, in search of what–a dream I'd carried for over thirty years, to live in France?

I leaned back in my seat as the jet climbed through the sky, closed my eyes as warm tears wet my cheeks–tears of relief.

Yes, I was doing it, giving myself something I'd wanted for so long.

I was on my way.

Fall 1961

I sat on the white chenille bedspread on my twin bed and listened as my sister Sharon lounged nearby with her friend Holly and they went over their first days in high school. I was still in junior high and wanted to hear all about their exciting new life.

They giggled about boys and compared their class schedules. Then Holly opened up her French I textbook and began reading out phrases. *Je t'aime,* I love you. That led to a new fit of giggling from the two of them. *Une chambre meublée,* which meant furnished room, also seemed funny. I, however, was not giggling. Those French words and sounds lit a spark and something inside me woke up and paid attention. I sat up straight and leaned in closer.

Holly pursed her lips and read on. *Un café au lait et un croissant, s'il vous plaît.* Coffee with milk and a croissant, please. When my sister and Holly moved on to other topics, I grabbed the book to look at the pictures and words. A waiter with a white napkin over his arm served coffee to people sitting at small tables at a sidewalk café in Paris. The Eiffel Tower loomed over the vast city. The geometric perfection of the Rose window of Notre Dame cathedral, old bridges over the Seine River–all the images seemed to jump off the page.

I held the book close and didn't want to give it back. Why did these sounds and these images pull me so? And when could I learn to speak this language that evoked something in me?

I'd heard French before, when my father told stories about his time in France during World War Two. Dad had studied French in South Dakota, from a teacher who had never heard French, so his accent made the words sound just like English. I loved his funny stories of how, while in France, when he tried to speak French, *s'il vous plaît* came out sounding like 'silver plate.'

I also could sense Dad's emotion when he talked about the French orphan Gilbert who Dad had tried to adopt and bring home with him to America. But the way that Holly had said these French words, no, that was something else.

Two years later, when I began my French studies, French became my favorite subject, by far. I'd stay up late to learn each word, to understand the accents, to memorize the irregular verb endings, to tuck each new piece of the language deep into myself, into a private place that was just my own. French and France became my own personal obsession.

In my 'inner French world,' I felt free and alive. In that world, I had no history of arguments with my critical mother, no boyfriend troubles, no confusion about my future. In that place I was certain of one thing. I would go to France and speak those thrilling sounds and my life would change for the better. I would express this tingling energy that French evoked in me.

I became the top student in French in my high school. Excelling in French became how I defined myself, my sense of identity. For the next five years, French continued to be the center of my private world. When I couldn't go abroad during high school summer programs, I became more riveted on doing my junior year abroad in college. I began saving for that time, tucking away money from summer jobs, part-time babysitting, theater ushering and typing jobs. From all that I earned, a little bit went into a savings account, just for that purpose.

3

*Life is what happens to us
while we're making other plans.*

Attributed to John Lennon and others…

La Vie Réelle: Real Life

Fall 1968

As a sophomore in college, I looked ahead to going to France the next year, for my junior year abroad. Then life took a different turn. My parents had just divorced, my father had moved across the ocean to Hawaii, and with all the personal turmoil, I was falling behind in my fast-paced college French classes at UCLA. But I still hung onto the hope that I could find a way to go to France.

In the midst of all the challenges that life seemed to be throwing my way, I felt confused and rebellious. I had a new boyfriend and turned away from my strict Catholic upbringing, going against all the rules I'd been taught for eighteen years.

By spring, I was pregnant. I would not be spending my junior year abroad in France. I would be married to a medical student, moving to San Francisco and having a baby.

A part of me was excited to be embarking on a new life, moving to a new city, married with a baby. That's what we girls were told was our destiny, after all, to be wives and mothers. But my secret, private part, the French part, mourned the loss of something that I'd cherished for more than five years, a quarter of my young life.

What will become of us, it whispered to me, as I watched bright purple stretch marks zigzag across my ever enlarging stomach each week. I struggled to adjust to my new life, to finding my way around a strange city, learning to cook and navigating the unknown waters of marriage.

I had experienced my first failure to achieve something I had longed for. It was as if a wave had carried my dream out to sea. I could still see it bobbing in the ocean, but stood helpless on the shore, with no way of reaching it. Its pull had no logical explanation in my real life, but I sensed it, like an underground stream that fed and nourished me.

During my first few months in San Francisco, as I tried to make new friends, I met another medical student's wife who was in Physical Therapy school and told me how she had gone to Germany for her junior year abroad.

She described how she had shipped a year's worth of her special hair and facial products over to Germany; God forbid that she might run out and have to buy something new and strange.

I nodded, as if I understood, but with wide eyes. I'd never had special hair and facial products in my life, not to mention a junior year abroad. As she prattled on, I burned with envy.

I wanted to be her, perfect and planned; my own life felt so out of control. As I sat with her, my recent marriage and protruding stomach screamed out that I'd committed the shameful sin of 'premarital sex.' Her condescending smile told me that she knew that.

Yet, in spite of my confusion and uncertainty, I was certain of one thing. I didn't want her as my friend. I had a mother who loved to shame me. I didn't need a friend who did that.

San Francisco, in the late sixties, was the center of the hippie culture, full of barefoot flower children wearing beads and tripping out. The women's liberation movement was in full swing, with the news showing women burning their bras in front of city hall downtown. In the midst of all this turmoil and change, I gave birth to a beautiful baby girl.

In the ensuing months, home alone with my baby daughter, I couldn't escape the emotions and thoughts that fell in on me. My young husband was off fulfilling his goal of attending medical school. I was facing the fact that the life I'd imagined for myself was gone.

I'd defined myself by being a top French student, by the plan of going to France. But now what? Who was I under that? I had no idea. Why was I so lacking in confidence? Why did I feel so ashamed and unworthy? Why, under an outer exterior that pretended that everything was all right, did I feel so lost and alone?

And what was I supposed to do about all my conflicting feelings about being married with a baby, when a part of me just wanted to rewind the movie and go back to being a carefree coed, going off to France for a year? I didn't know who to talk to. No one else seemed to be asking those questions.

It began to dawn on me that I'd arrived at 'adulthood,' married with a baby, completely unprepared for life. My husband and I had no skills for resolving conflicts. My parents' model of relationship offered no help in that department. They'd just divorced, after twenty-six years of arguing and unhappiness.

It felt like I'd arrived to go snow camping in the Sierras, wearing a short black dress and high heels. How in the world could I fill in the giant gaps in my education for how to function in life? While I disliked my mother, I loved my father, but he lived across the ocean in Hawaii and was getting remarried.

My sister, my best friend, now lived five hundred miles away. Sometimes, desperate for our connection, we'd steal a precious hour talking on the phone. But then my husband would yell at me when the phone bill came.

How could the most important part of life have been left out of over fourteen years of a 'good' education? Why had no one asked the important questions, the answers to which I so desperately needed? What if, instead of memorizing dates of wars, times men killed each other and occupied each other's land in endless power struggles, we'd learned some actual useful information?

Information such as skills in relationships, communication and intimacy, parenting, sexuality, confidence and self-worth, for starters. I couldn't talk to my husband about any of this. He was busy studying and going to school. And what was I to do about my cherished desire to live in France?

I'd stop at the mailbox on the way to the Laundromat, my daughter in her stroller and the laundry stuffed into the basket on the back, hoping for a postcard from my good friend Susan, who was doing her junior year abroad in Germany.

I'd stare at a castle or a medieval village and read about her adventures, then come back to the diapers spinning in the dryer and my baby daughter gurgling and smiling at me. Europe was a place in fairy tales, a fantasy.

I had two lights in my world at that point, the first, my delightful baby daughter who grew and blossomed in front of my eyes. The other, more secret light was my passion for French that I held onto like a life raft.

I'd save up money to head to the international newsstand and purchase a coveted French *Vogue*. At night, while Michelle slept, I'd then pore over the articles, translating words I didn't recognize with my worn, thick French dictionary. I'd sneak off to a French movie at a foreign film venue, watching the subtitles, listening to the sounds, struggling to understand the dialogue. Pushing Michelle in her stroller through the crowds at Fisherman's Wharf, when I'd hear tourists speaking French. I'd dawdle, lean in and listen.

As the years passed, I took French classes, listened to tapes and joined conversation groups. My personal life took twists and turns. I returned to college to complete my degree, gave birth to my second daughter and then went through a divorce after eleven years of marriage.

All through those years, the two constant lights in my life continued to be my delight in my daughters and my love of French. Even when I had to ignore French for years, it took just a spark to reignite it and I'd be off on a new round of learning and exploring the world of the language. It was like a thread that wove through my life, under and over, in and out, but always there.

When I was thirty-three, I managed a month-long trip to France. I'd only known the country through pictures in books as I had studied the language. As a friend and I explored France–from the Alps, to the Mediterranean, to Normandy and of course, beginning and ending in Paris–I experienced the wonder of uttering those melodic sounds to secure hotel rooms, to order food from rude Parisian waiters and to visit castles in the Loire valley.

The worry that I might be disappointed by finally visiting the country I had coveted for so long, turned out to be ridiculous. Instead, the private, French part of me breathed and laughed, sighed and spoke. I treasured this magical and mystical piece of myself even more because of all the time I had waited to experience her.

Eleven more years passed before, at age forty-four, I found my way to France for the second time. But during those years,

I had continued to work to increase my strong foundation in the language. By then, my eldest daughter was married and my youngest in college.

On that month-long trip, I fulfilled my wish to explore France with a rail pass, free and alone. One day, as I climbed to the top of an ancient tower in St. Malo, with an older woman I had met, a couple of teenage boys rushed past. I heard them comment that they had just passed "*une vielle femme et une jeune femme.*" An old woman and a young woman. I was the 'young woman.' In my exuberance and excitement, my younger self must have been beaming out through my skin and eyes and those young boys sensed it.

Over the next six years, I traveled to France six more times. I was by then writing articles about France, including stories about my father and his time there during World War Two. At the 50th anniversary of D-Day in 1994, I placed an ad in the local paper, looking for the French orphan, Gilbert DesClos, who my father had tried to adopt in 1944. I was doubtful that I would find him, but the very next day, Gilbert read the ad, and got in touch.

The moment I met Gilbert, I understood that one of the main reasons I'd been drawn to learn and to know French was so that I could find him and tell him that my father had never forgotten him. Those words meant everything to Gilbert, who had never been adopted. I tell this incredible story in my memoir, *Reunion, La Réunion, Finding Gilbert.*

After our reunion, I returned to France to visit Gilbert and his family many times, including taking members of my own family to France for a '*grande fête*'; everyone in Gilbert's village turned out to celebrate, even the mayor. The DesClos family also traveled to California for a two-week visit filled with dinners, picnics, visits to San Francisco, Hollywood, Universal Studios and lots of family fun.

My frequent visits, my relationship with Gilbert and my writing about France could have satisfied my hunger for the place. But instead, it just increased the longing I had always carried, to *live* there. Was it possible to fulfill such a deep desire—thirty years late? Would it be selfish and self-centered to take that time for myself?

My sister was struggling with her brain tumors and another close friend was dying of cancer, reminding me of the fragility of life and the importance of 'seizing the day.' What a gift it would be, at the age of fifty, to step back from my life, take stock of the successes and the failures, and look ahead at the time that was left.

What would it be like to allow that nineteen-year-old self, who'd had to quash that long-ago dream, to surface and to find a voice?

I didn't know. But as the plane winged its way east, I settled back into my seat, content that I'd just set off on a pilgrimage to France to find out.

4

For a journey without challenge, has no meaning;
one without purpose, has no soul.
Phil Cousineau, *The Art of Pilgrimage*

L'Arrivée: The Arrival
November 4, 1999

Bleary eyed and groggy, I stumbled into the futuristic glass
walkways of Charles De Gaulle airport. After retrieving
my bag, I lumbered onto the RER train to Paris, to my hotel
in the Latin Quarter. Even though I'd done my best to pack
light, I juggled a purse, a shoulder bag bulging with laptop and
camera, and one small rolling bag. At my stop, after dragging
my bags up the stairs, I arrived at the exit turnstile.

In the narrow space of the turnstile, as I struggled to pass
through, the automatic doors closed inward with a 'shush,'
trapping my arm carrying the laptop/camera bag.

Completely stuck and helpless, squeezed into the turnstile
doors, I let out a pained yelp of 'help' (in English). This caused
some commotion, not to mention that I blocked the way out
for the people behind me. After a few embarrassing moments,
some kind American tourists extricated me from those terrible
pinching doors.

So much for my fantasy of a cool and suave entrance into the City of Lights, *'La Journaliste Américaine.'* I slunk up the stairs and out onto the busy thoroughfare of *Boulevard St. Michel.* Students and workers bustled past on their way to somewhere in their daily lives. Whereas I had just stepped *out* of my daily life, heading for something a bit more elusive.

I stopped and breathed in the cool November air. I had arrived, in Paris. I wanted to kiss the ground, but instead stood still and took in the scene around me. Across the street, tall wrought iron gates enclosed the Jardin de Luxembourg. Overhead, a gray sky threatened rain and next to me, the magazine kiosk on the corner offered the latest issues of *Paris Match* and other French periodicals.

Each time I landed in France, I felt the same exhilaration that I had just traveled back through time, to this enchanted place that had lived only in my imagination for so long, the place in the French I textbook all those years ago. But it was real and I was here. And this time I was staying for a while.

I had arranged a hotel just off *Boulevard St. Michel* for my first night and after dropping off my bags, set off to *Notre Dame Cathedral,* just across the Seine. Dim purplish light filtered through the giant Rose window and candles flickered around the statues of the saints. It felt as if the hallowed space held all the prayers and sacredness of the centuries, ready for me to just breathe it all in.

A priest was saying the noon mass and as he droned on in French, I was reminded of my childhood, when the priests recited the mass in Latin. I lit a candle and said a prayer for the journey I had embarked on. As I sat in the pew, listening to the mass, I pondered the eight months that stretched out in front of me, open.

I wanted to fulfill my longing to become fluent in French. I couldn't explain logically why that mattered to me. Spanish was the practical language for someone living in California.

But it had mattered to my nineteen-year old self, and I was here to give her a chance to come out of cold storage, deep inside of me, where she'd been hiding for thirty years. She had wanted to be fluent in French. I still wanted that. Those were reasons enough for me.

I wanted to follow my hunch about living in Aix-en-Provence, in the south.

"Why not Paris," so many people had suggested? "Such an exciting, vibrant city."

Yeah, why not Paris? How to sort out my true desires from conflicting thoughts and feelings? I wasn't used to so many choices and to such a blank slate, both wonderful and at the same time, a bit terrifying.

What if I wasted the whole time wandering, never finding a home and after all my waiting, this experience let me down?

I breathed in the fragrance of incense in the cathedral and let the echoing voices around me soothe me and quiet my too busy mind.

Just trust, I heard from somewhere deep inside me.

Yes, that's what I needed to do. Just trust.

Orange and gold fall leaves danced and swirled in the chilly wind as I headed back across the Seine. I pulled my wool shawl around me, enjoying moving my body through space after the confinement of the long flight. I could feel myself landing, step by step, and coming into the present moment, in Paris.

In the evening, after a light meal and a hot bath, I tumbled into the clean, starched sheets in my hotel room and slept. The next morning, the hotel breakfast of fresh *pain, croissant*, butter, jam and tea provided me with warmth and sustenance to head out for the day ahead. Map in hand, I set off to explore the *quartier*.

My budget couldn't handle the luxury of staying in a hotel beyond a single night, so I staked out a youth hostel where my daughter Heather, who was teaching English in Belgium for a few months, joined me for three nights. We laughed with our two other roommates, lined up for the shower room down the hall, and gathered with the other guests for the group breakfast in the basement.

Being with Heather felt like a gift. We'd been to Paris together twice before, staying in hotels, and I found myself wishing that this time we'd had that luxury, with a bathroom and a space all our own. But, at twenty-four, she didn't mind the youth hostel and we met lots of interesting people of all ages, from all over the world. Even people my age were off on adventures and also on a budget. Maybe I wasn't so weird after all?

After Heather left to go back to Belgium, I looked for another place to stay. I had two prospects, one free and the other, a dormitory for international students and teachers, which allowed for longer stays.

The free option was the famed English language bookstore, Shakespeare and Company, just across the Seine from *Notre Dame*. The eccentric owner, George Whitman, had run the place since the nineteen fifties and had a reputation for inviting writers to stay, free of charge, in exchange for a few hours of helping out at the store. Curious, I headed in to look around. When I located the owner, we chatted a bit and true to form, he invited me to stay.

I wandered around the labyrinth like rooms, crammed with books in every nook and cranny. I saw several single beds tucked in around the bookshelves, with rumpled sheets and bedding that looked like it all hadn't been washed in a while. One of those would be my space if I took him up on his offer.

I was still overcoming jet lag and feeling quite open and vulnerable in my new space of freedom. But, as I looked around at the bustling activity of the bookstore and back at the small beds, I realized that I wasn't up for the challenges that his offer would entail.

I was on a budget, true. If I were twenty, I'd probably leap at the chance. But at fifty?

Afraid of offending Whitman by not accepting his offer, I slunk out of the bookstore when he was busy with a customer. When I went back weeks later to browse, he didn't recognize me, which was a relief. I'd heard that he yelled or threw books at people if he got upset.

I found the dormitory down a side street and though I felt a little awkward and out of place as I checked in, the staff were friendly and polite. They assigned me a two-person room to myself, probably because I was the age of everyone's mother. As I wrestled my luggage up to the fifth floor, huffing and puffing, I couldn't help thinking that the students, unlike me, could carry their bags up those five flights of stairs with ease

The tiny room reminded me of my dorm room at UCLA, all those years before: two twin beds with a narrow space between. The one small window looked out on another building and its dirty white curtain may not have been washed since my own days in college. But the room had a private shower and included breakfast, for a total price tag of eighteen dollars, a fraction of the cost of a hotel room.

As I settled in, I discovered that the light didn't work and that there were no towels. Back down the five flights of stairs I went, to inquire about buying one, only to discover that on Sundays, the stores were all closed.

"*Désolé.*" Sorry, the petite young woman behind the desk shrugged.

Oh well. Back up the stairs to improvise with a t-shirt as a towel. The water in the shower dripped out in spindly streams, but was good and hot, so I stood under it for at least twenty minutes, letting the heat seep into my scalp.

When I awoke the next morning, in a fog of jet lag, I stared around at the dingy, dirty room and wanted to pull the covers over my head. This was not how I'd imagined it would be, my first days in Paris.

Shivering, I got dressed and headed to the dining room, where students chatted in clusters, at various tables. I sat alone, shy and feeling like a combination of the new kid at school and the out of place parent. Breakfast consisted of a rather stale baguette, butter, jam, coffee and some kind of Tang-flavored orange drink. But considering the price tag, I was happy.

In the rush to leave California, I'd neglected to buy the right adapter for my new laptop, so was frantically trying to figure out what to do, as my battery continued to run down. I didn't even understand computer technology in English and now had to discuss it in French. As I set off to purchase an adaptor and a towel and a few other things, the chilly, damp air cut right through the light wool cape I wore. Who knew that the City of Light could be so cold and dark in November? I'd only ever visited it in the summer.

As I shivered my way along the boulevards, I noticed how fast I walked compared to everyone else; I slowed my pace. Later, as I waited in line at the post office to mail something back to California, I realized I also needed to develop patience. Things took time in France. The wine aged slowly and the lines at the post office moved slowly too. No use getting upset. It would just take longer then.

I found an Internet café where I purchased time to do emails by the half hour. I couldn't use my laptop, so had to use their computers, which presented a challenge since the French keyboard is different from our American one. A and Q are reversed, also Z and W, with M and various punctuation in different places. So typing a simple email took a while to go back and correct all my errors.

I also purchased a phone card at a *Tabac* and called Gilbert and Huguette and let them know I'd arrived. It was comforting to hear their voices.

In spite of the cold, I stayed out most of the day, avoiding that small, dark room in the hostel. I warmed up in a cozy café with some *soupe à l'onion* at lunchtime and later, for a *grande crème décafféinée.*

By late afternoon, I still had not located an adapter for my computer and dragged along *Boulevard St. Germain*, on my way back to the dormitory.

As I passed a busy shop window, a bookstore filled with student supplies–notebooks, textbooks, pencils and pens, I happened to glance up. Printed on the background wall of the display were three words: *Croyez-en-soi.* Believe in yourself.

People shuffled by, cars honked, but I stood still. It was as if a silent hand reached out, tapped me and whispered, *"Hey, you–the American lady who is wondering about this plan she hatched. Believe in yourself. That's all you have to do. Just those three words. Let the rest go. It's really that simple."*

I searched the window display for the reason those words were there, but couldn't find one. And what was the chance that I would be walking by and just happen to look up at the exact right second and see those words?

I'd always thought of belief as something held out for someone else. Belief in God, belief in something. But belief in *myself?*

But the phrase wasn't "Believe in yourself." It was *"Croyez-en-soi."* The words were *in French*, the language I'd adopted so long ago and which now pulled me in and held me close.

Standing there alone, shivering and staring into that shop window, I felt safe. I knew that this was the key to navigating the next few weeks of twists and turns on my way to having a home in France.

The words felt like my life preserver and I could hold on tight. It was my reassurance that there was a plan much bigger than I could see, way beyond what my little mind could figure out, that was in motion and I was in for one hell of a ride. If–and of course this was the giant 'if'– I could *"croyez-en-soi."*

Could I? Well, I had done it enough to get this far, to be standing there at this shop window as night fell on Paris. So just maybe I could. I pulled out my pocket journal and wrote down the words. Back at the dormitory, I stood again under the spindly shower stream, dried off with my new towel, then crawled under the thin blanket and looked up at the dirty curtain on the window.

I thought back on my day, how I'd wandered around Paris, drinking in the place and breathing in the language. English thoughts spoke to me inside my head as the world swirled around me, in French.

Then the three words. A bridge from how it was, to how I hoped and believed it could be.

Croyez-en-soi.

5

...if the journey you have chosen is indeed a pilgrimage,
a soulful journey, it will be rigorous.

Phil Cousineau, *The Art of Pilgrimage*

Croyez-en-soi

I kept those words close to me all during the next day as I
made my rounds to the Internet café again to check email
and to meet an old friend for coffee. As I got onto the bus, my
arm got caught in the door and once again, I yelped out loud
in pain. I couldn't help but wonder what it was with me and
automatic closing doors in Paris.

Then I saw the shocked faces of the people in the bus. *Ooh,
là, là*–I'd just committed a big *faux paux*. It seemed that people
just didn't cry out, at all there, for whatever reason. So I not
only stood out because I was a tall American who walked too
fast. I stood out because, at that moment, I was a very *loud* tall
American.

After I hurried off the bus, I realized that I'd lost my favorite, warm gloves. *How could you have done that?* The mean
voice inside my head sounded like my mother.

At lunchtime, in a sidewalk café near the Jardin de Luxembourg, I ordered a *'demi-pichet du vin'* with my *'poulet,'* chicken,
thinking I had ordered a *little* pitcher of wine. After a shocked

discussion with the waitress, it turns out that a '*quart-pichet*,' a quarter pitcher, is what I should have ordered. '*Un demi-pichet de vin*,' a half pitcher of wine, is actually a *lot* of wine.

But I had a great view of people passing by and my journal. Filtered sunlight brightened the cold November day. I sat, sipped, wrote and people watched as I drank most of that wine all by myself. After a strong '*grande crème décafféinée*,' I wobbled off on the rest of my errands.

I'd heard that The American Church, on the Left Bank, provided a bulletin board where people could post housing and job opportunities. I wanted to check it out, on the slight chance that I was supposed to stay in Paris. I was about 90% sure that I wanted to go Aix-en-Provence, but thought I'd go and look anyway.

I found the church and did see some promising notices, but still sensed a pull to go south. As I walked back to the dormitory, I heard the words from the bookstore echoing in my mind. *Croyez-en-soi.*

I hadn't managed to find an adaptor, and my computer battery continued to drain. In desperation, that evening I found myself on a bus headed across Paris to a mega-store. As I stared out the bus window at unfamiliar stores and darkened streets, I realized how at home I felt in the 5ᵗʰ arrondissement, the Latin Quarter, the area I'd just left behind. *Boulevard St. Michel, Boulevard St. Germain*, and *Notre Dame Cathedral* all seemed like old friends. I dreaded going to a strange neighborhood in Paris, at night.

The exhaustion of jet lag that always hit in the late afternoon made me want to curl up in a ball. I shivered both from the cold and from the twinges of malaise stirring in my stomach. I wasn't just out on a limb–I couldn't find any branches at all, just air.

Sighing, I rested my head against the cold glass of the bus window. I hadn't imagined it being this hard, so far from home and all that I knew.

You're doing so great.

I sat up and looked around, startled. Who was talking to me, in English? I'd never heard that voice before, inside my head. Because it *was* in my head. The seat next to me was empty and the world around me was happening in French. It went on.

Look at you, on a bus, going across Paris to a neighborhood you don't know, to try to find an adapter for your computer. You barely understand computers in English and now you're conversing about them in French. You're amazing.

I looked out the window again at the unfamiliar storefronts passing by and let a soothing sense of calm wash over me. I *was* courageous. I hadn't though of it that way.

With renewed determination, I located the giant store and snagged a person to help me. After hearing about my problem, he thought I needed a part that was going to cost about a hundred dollars, but he wasn't sure. Something told me to wait, even though that meant I'd just made a useless trip across Paris.

I caught the bus again, back across town, back to the relief of my known neighborhood. As I hopped off, so happy to be again where I knew my way around and energized that I had survived that challenge, I noticed a store with the small rainbow-colored apple computer sign.

Try there, said the helpful voice.

I ran up the stairs, out of the cold. A young, earnest looking man stood behind the counter. Computer parts bulged out of every nook and cranny on the shelves behind him. As I explained my situation, he smiled a slight smile, possibly at my American accent. But he understood, turned and grabbed a little gizmo off the shelf. Ten dollars. *Voilà!* My adapter.

I felt such relief and validation that I'd trusted not to buy the other one that I fairly skipped down the stairs as I headed back to the dormitory.

With my laptop now charging, I relished the joy of writing down my thoughts as the sounds of Andrea Bocceli belting out "Per Amore" filled the tiny space. My laptop felt like an old friend, there to help me as I eased into my new life in France.

The difficulty and challenges of those first few days in Paris took me by surprise. On previous visits, I had been on vacation, just a short trip, staying in hotels, secure in the knowledge I'd be heading home to my stable life in just three weeks.

It had been as if I was on a rubber band that stretched out from California to France and back, and I was just along for the ride, a gentle forward and back, all lined up in advance, sure in its trajectory.

This time, though, I wouldn't be going home for eight months, and the future yawned open in front of me, both tantalizing in the freedom it offered and terrifying in the uncertainty it contained.

Was I a fool to have followed my yearning to come to France to live? Would this uncertainty pass? I didn't know. I so hoped it would.

As I looked around the dingy dormitory room, I heard the friendly voice again.

Yes it will pass.

And I remembered my new mantra. *Croyez-en-soi.*

Good. I'd just have to stay tuned.

To cheer myself up, I listed all the things I loved about being in Paris, alone, on a cold November night, at age fifty.

I loved that the streets were filled with people day and night and that I was safe, as a woman, walking alone. I loved meeting new people and the kindness of the people at the front desk at the dormitory. I loved being able to take the bus or metro to get all over the city, so different from my life at home, out in the country, living on an apple farm.

I loved that I was strong enough to face all this alone, a foreign culture, language, and, except for a few known blocks of the Latin Quarter, a huge, strange city.

I sensed that the challenges I was facing were the gargoyles that guarded the gate to something great for me, but I had to be willing to give up all the comforts of the familiar to access it.

And lastly, I loved the new, kind voice that seemed to be right there when I needed it, offering encouragement. And my new French mantra, *croyez-en-soi*.

6

Gilbert Desclos, Mon Frère Français:
Gilbert Desclos, My French Brother

The next day, I caught the #21 bus across Paris to the Gare
Saint Lazare train station, to catch the train to Normandy
to visit my French 'family,' Gilbert and Huguette Desclos.

Gilbert's birthday was a day after mine and we were going
to have a joint celebration. I would also be there for Veteran's
Day, November eleventh.

As I got off the train in Caen, I spotted Gilbert smiling
and waving in the crowd. He greeted me with the special four
kisses, reserved for close family, then took my bags from me as
we walked to his car.

My dad would have been waiting for me at the station like
that, and I was struck, as I was every time I visited Gilbert, by
how similar they were. It was as if seven-year-old Gilbert had
soaked up Dad, body and soul, from the five months they'd
spent together in Normandy. Visiting Gilbert gave me back a
piece of my father, in addition to a new member of my family,
a *French* family member. Both were precious gifts.

"*Ca va, Diane?*" he asked. "Everything going well?" Gilbert pronounced my name in the French way, "Deeaahn." The
fact that none of Gilbert's family spoke English relieved any

shyness I may have had about whether or not I spoke perfect French. I was glad I'd had almost a week to let my brain begin to readjust to French before my visit with them.

At their home, Gilbert's wife Huguette greeted me with the same four kisses. Elliott, the dog bounded up and demanded a pat. The cat snoozed on the couch. We drank an aperitif, *kir royale*, champagne with a drop of kir liqueur, then sat down for one of Huguette's delicious meals. *Coquille St. Jacques*, with salad, cheese, bread and fruit, served with a light white wine.

After dinner, they shooed me off to bed. My jet lag was still real. Up the creaky, narrow, wooden stairs to the bedroom where I always stayed, which seemed so comfortable and familiar, clean and cozy, like *my* room, in France. I was a little long for the bed, but stretched out sideways, I drifted off between the crisp, clean sheets that Huguette had carefully ironed.

The next day was Veteran's Day and Gilbert, who had served in the military in Vietnam, took part in an honor guard ceremony. It started with champagne at eleven, then a parade and speeches. Afterwards, we joined a few other veterans and their wives for a special luncheon. The afternoon went like this.

Ca a commencé, it began:

1:00, *Foie gras avec champagne*: foie gras with champagne

1:45, *un plateau de fruits de mer–huîtres, crevettes, crabe, vin blanc:* a platter of fresh seafood, oysters, shrimp and crab, with chilled white wine

2:30 *Glace avec Calvados*: sherbet and hard apple cider, to clear the palate

2:40 *Veau, jambon et fromage avec tomates et pommes de terre, vin rouge*: the main course, veal, ham and cheese, with tomatoes and potatoes, and red wine

3:15 *Salade, frommage, vin rouge*: salad, cheese, red wine

3:40 *la table débarrassée*: everything cleared away, the table cleaned off

3:50 *champagne et dessert:* champagne and dessert–some kind of a fluffy, light creation with a fruit sauce

4:15 *café et chocolate:* coffee and chocolates

4:20 *champagne:* more of it

4:30 *au revoir:* with two kisses all around.

Which just made me wonder, as always, how *did* the French stay so slim and trim after sitting down to a three and a half hour lunch, including all that wine and champagne? *Un miracle.* But I relished it all: my brain got soaked with French, my body with delicious food, champagne and wine, and my soul with *l'art de vivre,* the French art of living. I was reminded, once again, to *slow down.*

To celebrate Gilbert's and my birthdays, their daughter Cathy and her sons Romain, fourteen, and Benoit, nine, joined us for dinner. Gilbert and I blew out the candles on the cake that Huguette had baked. Between us, we shared one hundred and fourteen years.

They gave me a purple scarf and gloves, which I was grateful to receive, especially after losing my favorite gloves. I had brought Gilbert some special family photos of my dad when he was young. He loved them, as he loved all things related to my father.

Gilbert called me *"notre petite Américaine,"* our little American, a joke, since I was tall like my father and towered over everyone. But it felt sweet to be teased and I knew that he loved that I resembled my dad. The first time I met Gilbert, he said that he recognized me because I looked so much like my father.

Before I left, Huguette repeated her invitation for me to stay with them for my eight-month sojourn. For a moment, I thought about how easy and comfortable that would be. But while I so appreciated her offer, I knew that I needed to find my own way on this journey, and to make sure I'd have solitary time to write. I would come and visit, I promised. Their love and support comforted me and provided me with a safety net.

7

We need to believe that there is something sacred
waiting to be discovered in virtually every journey.
Phil Cousineau, *The Art of Pilgrimage*

Suivre Les Points: Following The Dots

B oosted by my visit to Normandy and the warmth and caring of Gilbert and Huguette, I took the train back to Paris
and checked back in to the dormitory. While I planned to head
south to Aix-en-Provence, I wanted to stay in Paris for a few
more days. I was watching for signs.

I was reminded of 'following the dots' in a children's color-
ing book, where you connect the dots to discover the image.
It was as if I was discovering a dot, taking a step, then looking
for the next dot, on and on, trusting that the picture would
eventually emerge. So far, the dots had been the words, *croyez-
en-soi*, the kind voice in my head, and the nurturing love in
Normandy.

I was looking for a sense of certainty that I was supposed to
go to Aix, rather than stay in Paris. That would be the next 'dot.'

That afternoon, I bought myself a long, black, wool coat,
the style worn by all the Parisian women I encountered on the

street. The saleswoman told me I looked '*très chic*' and the coat felt cozy and warm as I headed out into the chilly evening. I had called a contact that a friend in California had given me and, after chatting for a few moments, was invited to a party that night. It would require a metro ride across Paris with a connection to an unfamiliar neighborhood, returning late at night, which made me nervous. But they assured me that it would be safe.

So I ventured out, took the metro, made the connection, and found the place. The party was in full swing when I arrived and I had fun chatting with an interesting assortment of folks from all over Europe, listening to French, English, German and a few other languages. The two ladies who hosted the party invited me to come back when I was next in Paris.

I found my way back on the metro, at eleven o'clock. The streets were full of people and in my black, chic coat and leather backpack purse, I blended in. As my new friends had promised, it was safe. I was also warm in my lovely, long coat for the first time since I had arrived.

Now that I had a new, heavy coat, I so needed to lighten my load. So the next day, I went through my luggage and threw away as many things as I could, wishing I could chuck it all.

That night, I walked to the Eiffel Tower, arriving just as snow began to fall. From the empty third floor observation deck, I pulled my coat around me and looked out at Paris, which was covered in a light blanket of snow. For once the vibrant city felt hushed and quiet.

I stood alone, with the air full of soft snowflakes, surrounded by all that steel jutting up into the sky. As I breathed in the cold air, I let in the wonder of being alive right that very moment, looking out over the snow covered streets of Paris.

I had been in France just twelve days and yet already felt so different. New desires were sprouting inside me like tiny spring shoots: to live a softer life, with muted colors, fuzzy, with less hard edges. I wanted to relax, laugh and smile way more. What if that was all I did in my new life? That would that be some kind of amazing.

As the snowflakes floated past the lights of the tower and disappeared, I sensed that yes, going south, to a smaller town and a warmer climate, life could be gentler, easier.

I'd found the next 'dot.' I knew, for certain, that my next step was to go south to Aix-en-Provence.

The following morning, I left the dormitory, bought my ticket and boarded the TVG, the fast train, for Marseilles, where I would connect to the local train to Aix.

As we glided through a snowy winter landscape, under gray skies, I was cozy in my coat and scarf. I was on my way to the south and that felt significant.

My laptop comforted me with its familiarity, like a little piece of home. Its warmth even made it seem to be alive in my lap, like a favorite cat. It also reflected my work in France: writing and self-expression and being free to travel and do that.

As the train sped through the French countryside, the sky turned from blue to gray, then blue again and the clouds moved away. When was the last time I had taken the time to watch clouds, especially as I whizzed along?

Villages passed by, the houses huddled together, with a church steeple in the center. I thought about my home and farm, back in California, surrounded by eight acres, full of fruit orchards and tall pine trees.

The time on the train allowed me to muse about my future, and what I wanted it to be. What if I could be way more welcoming and giving in my life and worry less? What if I only did what made me smile or laugh, or what made others smile or laugh: only what generated joy?

I celebrated what I already had: excellent health, healthy relationships full of love, with family and friends. I was beginning to relax into the rhythm of France and into the notion that my most important job was to remember to thoroughly enjoy every single moment.

The train glided along, no rattling or shaking, just smoothness itself. I snuggled down into my coat, stuffed my scarf into a soft pillow against the cold glass of the window and dozed off. When I awakened, sunlight streamed through the clouds as we pulled into the Gare St. Charles, in Marseille.

I found the connection to Aix and hopped onto the small, rural train. As we rattled along the tracks, I realized that in spite of my visit to Aix, six months before, I couldn't remember how long it took to get there, or where to disembark. An older woman sitting nearby looked kind, so I posed those questions to her. In our conversation, I mentioned that I was going to live in Aix for eight months.

She looked me up and down, my coat, my suitcase and carry on and seemed to get alarmed.

"Do you know anyone in Aix?" she asked,

Non, I responded.

"Do you have a place to stay?" she asked.

Non, pas encore, I answered. Not yet.

Mon Dieu! Eyes wide, she pulled out a card. "Please call me if I can help you. Please come and stay with me if you need to."

I thanked her for her kindness, but reassured her that I would be all right. I did keep her card, though, tucked inside my wallet. Just in case. She motioned for me when the train was nearing Aix, then stood and waved as I walked away. I waved back. So much for the notion of the unfriendly French!

I couldn't remember how to get to the *centre ville,* so just followed the crowd with my rolling bag. As I approached *Cours*

Mirabeau, the main street with its giant fountain, I remembered where I was and felt a thrill to be back. Within a few minutes, I found the hotel where I'd previously stayed, *L'Hôtel du Globe*.

My hotel was located just minutes from the central plaza with the clock tower, so once I'd dropped my bags, I set off up the street to find it again. On the way, I passed a toy store and went in to look for a book for my grand daughter. The owner of the shop, a British man, chatted with me about Aix and my plans. I told him I was looking for an apartment and he mentioned a group that met once a week for coffee, called AAGP, the Anglo-American Group of Provence.

The Anglos and Americans met for coffee to take a break from French and to chat in English and the local French came to practice their English. I thanked him and wrote down the information. The group met on Thursday mornings. I'd just missed it, but I'd definitely be there the following Thursday.

Even though I knew no one, I was happy to be back in Aix. It felt so right.

I walked for hours, exploring the town, before sipping a *grande crème décafféinée* at a café in the filtered sun, grateful for my warm coat against the cold *mistral* wind of the south.

My inner world, the thoughts inside my head, occurred in English. The world around me, the outer world, spoke French. I found the challenge both exhilarating and, at times, exhausting. It's what I'd wanted, what I'd come to have, yet I was reminded that even those things we want are not always easy.

Hundreds of birds, creating a chorus of chattering, greeted me as I walked down the grand tree-lined street, *Cours Mirabeau*. On a side street, I stumbled upon the *Monoprix* supermarket where I purchased small glass pots of rich lemon and vanilla yogurt. In the days ahead, I bought apples, kiwis and carrots at open markets. Bakeries provided tiny quiches, tarts, *pain au chocolats* and sandwiches for lunch and dinner. As I wandered around Aix, the many hours of walking allowed me to enjoy it all and still fit into my jeans.

The chilly night temperatures meant that I could store the yogurt and fruit on the ledge outside my second story hotel window all night, then enjoy it for breakfast. As much as I enjoyed my tiny hotel room, I missed the simple comfort of being able to brew a cup of hot tea.

In one of those first few days, as I sat at a café, I heard the James Taylor song, "Fire and Rain," playing in the background. I'd always found that song moving and started to cry, but didn't want anyone to see.

Somehow I hadn't anticipated the tender vulnerability of being suspended in time, between lives, till I found a place to settle. Everyone around me had a life. I had left my old life behind and hadn't created my new one yet, so I was on the outside looking in.

Back again in my tiny hotel room, I fretted about money—so many nights in a hotel were not in the budget. *Since when, is it a problem to be staying in a hotel in the south of France?* my wise voice offered.

True. I sensed that my job was to learn to relax and to enjoy it all, even this beginning, unsettled time.

8

Stolen moments of contemplation
are the grace notes of a pilgrimage...
Phil Cousineau, *The Art of Pilgrimage*

Aix-en-Provence

An early snowstorm brought big, fat snowflakes, a foot of snow, and freezing temperatures that shut down the town. My shoes got soaked, walking around in it; I didn't have boots.

The morning after the storm, a Sunday, I wandered through the deserted and quiet streets, stepping over fallen branches, marveling at the transformation a blanket of snow had created in my new town. Everything was shut up tight on the central *Place de la Mairie*, except a teashop. Light glowed from inside and the sign said *Bienvenue*, Welcome.

The snow had soaked through my shoes and frozen my toes inside my wet socks. Towards the back of the shop, a crackling fire blazed; next to it was a large, soft armchair and I sank into it. A friendly waitress welcomed me and wanted to practice her English and at that moment, I was relieved to speak my native tongue.

I ordered a pot of Darjeeling Tea, took off my wet socks and shoes and wiggled my toes in front of the warm fire, grateful that no one seemed to notice. I didn't want to make any more *faux pas* and annoy the French sensibility. I took out my journal and began to write.

I was discovering the power of spending time in a culture that was not my own, in a language not my own, to find out who I was beyond the cultural definition of American, Californian, with the parents I had, the childhood I had, and the ideas about myself that I formed when I was young. Not to mention my adult roles of mother, wife, ex-wife, businesswoman, writer. Beneath all those, who was I really?

As I sipped my hot tea with milk and sugar by the fire in the 17th century building, I thought about how living what had been a buried dream was taking me to places that only it could take me. And it wasn't logical. I didn't like smoking and yet I was living in the land of Marlboros and Gauloise cigarettes. My clothes and my hair stunk from the smoke, but what had pulled me to France was beyond such things as my likes and dislikes.

The few people I'd chatted with since I'd arrived all had the same reaction.

"You came here alone, not knowing anyone?" They seemed to think that I was crazy? Had I been crazy? Well, so far, I was also discovering a sense of courage and power in staying centered in the midst of finding my way.

Even with all the challenges, being in Aix spoke to my heart and called me forward. Maybe I couldn't explain that, but I could trust. I could believe in myself. I could *croyez-en-soi*.

After my pot of tea, and an hour of writing, I ordered a bowl of rich tomato soup, which came with a crispy baguette. Oh the pleasure of the warm soup and the welcoming fire. I'd found a piece of my home right there in my new town.

It seemed that if I kept ordering things, spaced out over time, I owned the comfortable chair and could stay and write.

So a glass of *rosé*, then a *chasson aux pommes,* a wonderful apple tart, took me through the afternoon.

I remembered the image of 'following the dots' as a process for discovering my new life. This teashop and the hours I spent there, cozy by the fire, felt like another reassuring dot for my new life in Aix.

Late in the afternoon, I headed back to the hotel, warm and happy. The waitress had reassured me that I would find an apartment soon. Something would come up. The next day, I'd begin that search in earnest.

Over the next week, I learned a lot about the challenges of looking for an apartment in Aix. The first, was that in a University town, where thirty thousand students had arrived for fall semester three months before, all the good places had been snatched up.

The second, was how naive I had been to think that I could breeze in and rent an apartment, just like that. But I was determined. I began calling places listed in the local paper, using a pay phone and a calling card. I chased all over town on foot for hours, to look at various places. Some were like dark caves, others too far out of town, or above a noisy bar, or had no windows. Aix had two tattoo parlors, one on each side of town and I looked at an apartment above each of them.

I also discovered that rental agents expected to be paid one extra month of rent for their services and landlords expected a large *'caution'* or security deposit. I was also supposed to supply bank statements showing accounts full of cash and letters from my employer.

In spite of all these obstacles, I could sense my home out there somewhere in Aix. It had sunlight, windows and a bathtub, was in the *centre ville,* so that I could walk everywhere and was affordable. It was a test to hold onto that belief in the face of all the hours I spent finding my way to dead ends or looking at ugly, dirty, uninhabitable places.

I found an Internet café and struggled again with the French keyboard to stay in touch with my family and friends. This café was a bar and many times would be filled with locals yelling for their favorite soccer team. Sometimes I'd just get an email ready to send and it would disappear.

"*Désolé*," the young man behind the bar would shrug, neither of us understanding why the email had disappeared.

In the meantime, I moved to another hotel, *L'Hôtel de France*, right next to my favorite bakery on a busy street, *Rue Espariat*. The hotel cost forty dollars a night, less than the other one, and while that was still over my budget, I had no choice. There was no youth hostel in Aix within walking distance to the town.

The bright light in this time of searching for a home was my visit to the Anglo-American Group of Provence, the AAGP meeting, the next Thursday morning. I'd come to France to speak French, but the relief of speaking English for two full hours was a gift. I asked for help in finding a place and my new friends agreed to let me know if they heard of anything.

I felt especially drawn to a woman named Maïté. We kept looking at each other and at the end got a chance to chat for a few minutes. She invited me to come over to her apartment the next day for tea.

From the very beginning, Maïté felt like a friend and a sister. She worked as a tourism guide, so enjoyed practicing English and we ended up speaking a mixture of French and English. She offered to let me use her phone to call about apartments and phoned her friends to see if anyone knew of a place. After a few lunches together, she even invited me to come and stay with her while I looked. I appreciated her generosity, but declined, thinking that surely, it couldn't take much longer to find a place.

For what would have been Thanksgiving in America, I took

the train north to visit my daughter Heather in Belgium.

I'd bought a second-class ticket, *deuxième classe*, for the trip to Paris, where I would change trains for Belgium. Being together in that moving space was a group experience that the French seemed to accept. The woman behind me had two smelly dogs, and the old woman across the aisle had her Walkman turned up so loud that we all had to listen to her music, which was luckily upbeat. Another woman blew her nose and sounded like some kind of a horn.

But I saw a group of four elderly women, possibly in their late seventies, traveling together, alone and relaxed. They sat across from each other at a table in their chic wool suits and shared a picnic, drank some wine and chatted as we sped along.

A young woman walked up and down the aisle, soothing her baby. I read, enjoyed a beer with my lunch, wrote on my laptop, strolled to the dining car for tea and then took a nap. All of which would have been impossible in a car.

In the station in Aix the morning I left, I saw a train worker give two kisses to each of his female co-workers and shake each of the men's hands as he came into work. I guessed that any less would have been to insult his co-workers, but I wasn't sure yet, still figuring it all out as I went along.

I was reminded of a scene I once witnessed in Avignon. Two groups of two elderly couples greeted each other in the town square, a total of eight people. With the permutations of each person having to greet each other with two kisses, it took a full ten minutes just to begin a conversation.

It all seemed very sweet, though, to take the time like that, with kisses, something we'd lost in America, if we ever had it at all, with our Puritan heritage and our rush to succeed. I especially enjoyed watching groups of young men, with tattoos and piercings, exchanging two kisses when they'd meet in the street.

In Belgium, Heather and I couldn't find a turkey for our Thanksgiving feast, but roasted a plump chicken, with sweet potatoes and a sort of stuffing. I even made an apple pie, rolling out the crust with a wine bottle. She gathered some young American friends and we celebrated together, far from home.

Traveling on the train up and back to see Heather, with many hours to ponder and to write, I realized that I was now at the point where I would have returned home after a vacation in France–twenty-five days. So now what? What would open out of staying here beyond the usual vacation visit comfort zone?

Vacations were usually planned out, without too many surprises. My life at that moment was one continuous surprise after another. I had wanted an adventure and I was having one, with a capital A.

Doing my junior year abroad thirty years late, the advantages were that I had some wisdom and could do whatever I wanted. The disadvantages seemed to be that no one handled all the legwork for me or provided a structure to make sure that I was okay. I had to provide that for myself, finding lodging, making friends and finding my way.

Sitting there on that train, I realized how my life at home was set up to make sure that I was comfortable and adequate at every turn. Here, however, I was inadequate at almost every turn. French was my second language and many times I missed whole portions of a conversation because I didn't know a word and everything after that went somewhere other than into my brain.

Being uncomfortable looked like not knowing when I would find an apartment, how much it would cost, and how to bring in some income during my stay. Would my money hold out?

I was metamorphosing into something new, no longer the old me and not quite the new me yet, either. I had to continuously remind myself to trust, to *croyez-en-soi.*

9

*Every time we move toward a significant goal, the world
has a tendency to throw terrific obstacles in our way.*
Phil Cousineau, *The Art of Pilgrimage*

Ma Nouvelle Amie Maïté:
My New Friend Maïté

B ack at the *Hôtel de France* on the *Rue Espariat* in Aix, I started each morning with a pot of yogurt in my room along
with some fruit, then stopped at the Paul bakery for a croissant.
The warmth and the aroma of all the delicious baked goods felt
comforting, like stepping into a friend's kitchen, and bolstered
me as I set out to continue my search for an apartment.

I'd only brought three books with me to France. One, *The
Art of Pilgrimage: The Seeker's Guide to Making Travel Sacred*,
by Phil Cousineau, had become my bible. It encouraged me
to keep looking for the deeper meaning in my journey. Another was a favorite metaphysical book, *The Wisdom of Florence
Scovel Shinn*, and the last, *How to Write a Movie in Thirty Days*.

I missed my extensive bookcase at home, not to mention
access to a library, so in my hours of walking, was delighted when I discovered the Institute of American Universities,
where students from America came for their semester abroad.

When I walked into its library, seeing the quiet space packed with books in English sent a thrill through my body. How I had taken a library for granted at home!

I checked out old favorites–Willa Cather, Mark Twain, and other American writers–and devoured them at night in my hotel room. My brain, willing to speak French all day, wanted to read English at night. Somehow, those books eased the sense of loneliness and isolation of my tiny hotel room.

As I walked down the street one day on the way back to my hotel, I heard my mind say, *They are going to start speaking English now. I just know that they are.* I'd long passed the comfortable twenty-five day mark when I would have returned to the safety and comfort of my home environment.

At that moment, I felt some compassion for my brain, which had functioned in English for fifty years. It wanted to have a bit of a temper tantrum, lie down in the narrow street, pound the pavement and scream, *That's it! No more French. Why won't they just speak English? I want to speak English again. That's what I know.*

Well, "they" weren't going to speak English. "We" were there to speak French, I told myself, as if I was talking to a two-year-old. A stop in at the bakery for a mid-afternoon lemon tart seemed to calm things down again.

I loved my hotel's location on the *Rue Espariat*, with the bells of *L'Église de St. Esprit*, the Church of the Holy Spirit ringing out the hours, the Paul bakery just doors from my hotel, and the main street, *Cours Mirabeau*, a short walk away. The sign on the Paul bakery told how they had been making their bread since 1889. My favorite was *une baguette à l'ancienne*, a crunchy loaf that tasted of its ancient roots. If I could have traveled back one hundred and ten years to the day they first began baking these loaves, I'm sure they would have had the same nourishing flavor.

But even with the bakery, the church bells and all fountains, I so longed to unpack my suitcase and settle into a little space of my own. I could then have a phone and Internet connection and use my laptop for emails, saying goodbye to the Internet café with the confusing French keyboard and yelling soccer fans.

Through the Institute of American Universities, I met a man who rented out an apartment to visiting students. He seemed kind and didn't require all the extra deposits that the other landlords wanted. In my desire to get settled, I looked at his apartment and said yes to it, before I even knew what I'd done. It did not have sunlight, windows and a bathtub. Well, it did have *some* windows. And it was *near* the center of town, though in an unfamiliar area.

The landlord offered to pick me up from the hotel to drive my things over. As if in a trance, I watched myself carrying my bags up the stairs to the apartment, putting away my things, hanging a few posters and setting out a white candle that I'd bought in anticipation of having a home. In the rush to be *chez moi*, at home, I hadn't stopped to really listen to myself, to be sure that it felt right.

That first night, after a bowl of soup and a shower, I got into the single bed and tried to sleep, but couldn't seem to shake a sense of malaise. The apartment was on the third floor, and I hadn't seen or heard anyone else around; it felt spooky. As the hours passed, I could not sleep at all. When the sun came up and didn't shine in the windows, I knew what I had to do.

I called the man and apologized to him, telling him in my best French, that the place was not a fit for me. I could pay him for the one night there, if he liked. I could sense his disapproval underneath his polite French, but knew down to my bones that I could not live in that place.

We agreed where to meet to return the key. I took down the posters, packed up the candle and my clothes, then hauled my luggage down the three flights of stairs and navigated it for the ten-minute walk across town to Maïté's apartment. I rang her bell, but she was out, so sat down on the front steps of her building to wait, my luggage and my few bags of new items splayed all around me. I was going to take her up on her offer.

She showed up an hour later and smiled when she saw me. When I told her what had happened, she told me that the apartment had been in the one bad area of Aix, where there was a lot of drug dealing. No wonder I'd been so uncomfortable.

I moved into her spare bedroom, unpacked my candle, put some clothes into the closet and sighed with relief.

One of my heroines had always been Annie Oakley, 'Little Sure Shot' they called her, the best shot in the west. When my daughter Heather was in second grade, she brought a book home about Annie Oakley and we read it together. When Annie was learning to shoot a rifle, she said, "When it felt right, I pulled." I remembered that story and used it to encourage myself to pay attention to what 'felt right,' which wasn't always logical, but wasn't *ever* wrong.

That night in the apartment reminded me to pay more attention to how things felt and to trust that. A few days later, I got offered free rent in a small apartment in exchange for taking care of a big house when the owners left on vacation. My logical mind jumped at the chance to live rent free, busily adding and subtracting lines of figures in my budget.

But when I went to look at it, I found that it was way out of town, so I wouldn't be able to walk everywhere. And the thought of staying alone in a giant house when the owners were away *didn't feel right*. So I thanked them, said no and continued my search.

Maïté and I got into a routine, where I would shop and cook us something–so thrilled to have a kitchen again–or she would. We both bought fresh fruit and vegetables at the open markets and brought home bread and treats from the bakery. Maïté seemed more Californian than French. She didn't smoke, ate healthy food and went to the gym.

When we were both tired, she'd speak French and I'd answer in English. She corrected my French and I did the same for her English—we both wanted to learn and improve. In her tiny kitchen, she'd say, *oh pardon* when we'd cross paths, a reminder of the French manners and sensitivity of respecting each other's personal space. Evenings, we'd chat after dinner, read or I'd call ads for places to live. Neither of us liked to watch TV.

The energy required to search for apartments day after day caught up with me and I came down with a bad cold. Maïté also caught it, so for several days, we lay in our rooms, coughing, sniffling and resting. We took turns making soup or bringing each other juice or hot tea as we limped along. We were already close friends, but during those days of being sick and stuck together in her apartment, we bonded even more and our friendship deepened.

After almost a week, she suggested we go to see a doctor, so we headed off to his office on *Cours Mirabeau*. That was an interesting glimpse into French culture. The doctor did not have a receptionist, but just his examining room off a waiting area. We took turns having him listen to our chests and he prescribed something from *la pharmacie* and that was that.

While I was coughing and sputtering and sounding a bit like a frog, I spoke to my eldest daughter Michelle, back in California. In a reversal of mother/daughter roles, she was worried that I was sick and hadn't yet found a place.

"Are you sure you want to stay? You could just come back," she suggested.

The fact that I'd rented my house for another seven months meant I couldn't come back, even if I'd wanted to, but I felt her concern.

"I'm sure," I told her. "I want to stay. Things should come together soon."

I had one close friend, Janna, who was back in California, to whom I could talk openly. She knew that I was at a low point and kept telling me to not give up. I held on, feeling her love and concern in English and the comfort of my new friendship with Maïté, in French.

Maïté and I recovered just in time to attend an English Christmas Carol gathering at a beautiful thirteenth century Gothic church, *St. Jean de Malte*. The church overflowed with people and candles flickered on the altar and along the walls. As I let in the music and voices and sang all the old familiar carols, waves of nostalgia washed over me and I couldn't stop tears from falling.

All fifty of my Christmases, had been in California, in English. Here I was in France, still without a home after six weeks. Maybe I was extra raw and vulnerable from having been sick, but I could hear my own doubts in my head. Would I ever find my place here, a quiet, sunny apartment where I could write? Or would that continue to stay just out of reach? Was I going to fail, after I'd risked so much to come?

After the carols, Maïté and I went out for a drink with a few of her friends. One of the friends, Barbara, mentioned that she knew of a possible apartment. It was in the *centre ville* and she thought it had sunlight and windows, though she wasn't sure about a bathtub. She would call her friend and get back to us. Maybe the silent prayers I'd said in that lovely church had paid off? It felt like a sign.

Two days later, I met the real estate agent outside the apartment. I liked the location, just off *Rue Espariat* with my favorite bakery, and close to everything. We walked up three flights of stairs to the door on the left. The big, rusty key turned in the lock and the door swung open. Sunlight blazed through tall windows in the kitchen and living room. In the center, the dining room, French doors opened to a tiny balcony. I turned the corner off the kitchen to the bathroom and saw a deep, old bathtub.

Sunlight, windows and a bathtub. I wanted to jump up and down, dance with glee and hug the real estate agent, but I knew that would just cause another cultural *faux paux.* So instead, I took in a deep breath and smiled at her.

"Yes. It's just what I've been looking for. I'll take it!" I said, in my best French.

10

What matters most on your journey is how deeply you see,
how attentively you hear, how richly the encounters
are felt in your heart and soul.
Phil Cousineau, *The Art of Pilgrimage*

Chez Moi en France: At Home in France

Not only was the apartment just what I'd hoped for, but because I was a friend of a friend, the agent and owner didn't require all the extra deposits, fees and paperwork. The one problem was that the apartment needed cleaning, so I wouldn't be able to move in for several days until they could find someone to clean it.

I was so eager to move in, that I asked the woman if I could clean it myself, for a slight reduction in the price of the first month. She seemed surprised, but agreed, so we wrapped up the deal, she gave me the key and prepared to leave.

"Bon courage," she said as she turned to leave, looking at the mess, then looking back at me. I'd learned that the term, *bon courage,* which translates literally as 'good courage' was reserved for times when the French thought you needed a little, or a lot, of extra encouragement.

"Merci," I responded. Yes, I did have my work cut out for

me. The two young men who had lived there before had left behind quite a mess. A year's worth of cigarette butts, dust and dirt, papers and trash, for starters. Luckily, I'd cleaned houses as a teenager, so I rolled up my sleeves and got to work.

Maïté loaned me a vacuum cleaner, mop, bucket, rags and cleaning supplies and by the end of the day, the tile floor, bathtub, kitchen sink and windows shined. I so loved my new place and somehow, cleaning it all that day made it my own.

The apartment was *meublé*, furnished. In a University town, however, this simply meant a couch, table, chairs and bed; the renter needed to provide the rest. Sheets, pillows, towels, kitchen towels, a dish drainer, forks, plates, cooking utensils–all the little things you take for granted in a home did not come with the apartment. Maïté loaned me a few plates, cups, forks and a pan so I had some basics to get started. She also gave me a blanket for my bed, but I would have to furnish the rest.

Without sheets and pillows, I couldn't yet sleep in my place, so I went back to Maïté's for one last night and we celebrated my good fortune. The next morning, we drove to the *Carrefour*, a giant *supermarché* where I could buy what I needed.

I pushed a huge cart around, gathering sheets, towels, pillows, dish soap, dish drainer and a few more dishes, not to mention groceries. As I searched the aisles for a broom, I realized that in all my years of French study, I'd never learned the word for broom. Maïté had wandered off, so I was on my own.

I asked a young man for help, acting out sweeping, but he thought I'd spilled something and was just about to call for "cleanup on aisle six" when I shook my head and said, *non, pour chez moi.* No, for my house.

Ah oui, un balai! He led me to the corner of the store where the *balais* were stashed. *Voilà!* I stuck the broom into my cart and pushed it back to the grocery area. The next challenge was laundry detergent. I found an aisle with various cartons of things, but couldn't figure out whether they were fabric softener or detergent or some other mystery product in a box. Luckily, Maïté, who'd spotted me because my broom handle stuck up high into the air, reappeared, and helped me sort that out.

I stocked up on staples: the small glass pots of yogurt that I loved, packages of soup, cheeses, mustard, tea, milk and sugar. I would continue to buy my fruits, vegetables and bread fresh in Aix.

We stuffed all my bags and the broom into every available inch of Maïté's tiny red car and headed back to *chez moi*. She helped me carry it all up the three flights of stairs and then sat down for a cup of tea, with milk and sugar, which we drank in the two cups she had loaned me. Ah, so sweet to be able to sit at my table, with my friend, in my new clean and lovely space.

We hugged goodbye and I began to put my home together. The sheets went onto the bed, with the pillow and pillowcase, the kitchen towels onto the rack by the sink, the new white plastic dish drainer next to the sink, and the bath towels in the bathroom. I unloaded all my groceries into the tiny fridge and put the staples into the cupboard. My special candle went to the center of the old pine table.

Later that day, I bought a geranium plant for the balcony, its bright red flowers looking perky right outside the glass. That night, I cooked some soup in my one pan, set out bread, cheese and wine, lit my candle and sat down for my first dinner *chez moi*. Then I took a long soak in my lovely deep bathtub, crawled into my bed with the new sheets and fell asleep smiling.

When I awakened in the morning, it took me a moment to remember where I was. Then I saw the sunlight streaming into the windows. Ah yes, I was *home*. In *France*! It had taken all my trust, but the apartment had been worth waiting for. It felt so right.

I'd imagined renting a studio, to save money, but the rent for an entire flat was not that much more, and I loved the sense of spaciousness as I walked between the sunny kitchen and the dining room, from the living room into the bedroom, tucked into the back. The living room couch was a *click-clack*–a word that resembled the sound the couch made when you converted it into a bed. That could come in handy for visitors.

Maïté's fiftieth birthday fell on December 20th, just days after I moved into my new home. She rented a hall and invited all her friends, providing music, food and wine. I knew a few people from AAGP, but mostly didn't know the guests, so shook hands and smiled as I made new friends. It was special to see Maïté surrounded by her family and special friends who wanted to celebrate her half-century mark.

As I sat in my metal folding chair and watched people out on the dance floor, I was struck by the idea that no one knew me. I had no history with these people who, all around me, were chatting, smoking, drinking and celebrating. Which meant that in this group, there wouldn't be any, 'that's just the way Diane is.' That gave me a ticket to be any way I wanted. Did I have the courage to try out new ways of being? These nice French people would never know.

So I got up and headed to the dance floor. I pushed myself to loosen up and move with the music, experimenting with ways of dancing, turning and reaching and *oh this was very fun*.

I even asked a few men to dance, letting the experience of freedom tingle through my body and out through my smiling face. By two in the morning, I was happily worn out from all that liberation and caught a ride home with one of my new friends. Maïté and many others stayed up till dawn, which, I was to learn, is a routine part of celebrating in France.

For the holidays, I caught the train to Paris and then Normandy to celebrate Christmas with Gilbert and Huguette and their family. Winter storms had disrupted many routes and the trains overflowed with travelers, but arriving at their home was, as always, familiar and comfortable.

A neighbor had given Huguette a fresh, plump hen, which she roasted for our Christmas dinner. Their daughter Cathy and her sons came over and we exchanged simple presents. For Huguette, I had chosen a hand embroidered tablecloth, bought at the open market in Aix. I gave Gilbert and Cathy warm scarves and the boys, some books. After dinner, we turned on the brightly colored lights on the tiny tree in the window.

Being with them again, I noticed how much my French had improved in the six weeks since my last visit. French was beginning to be another channel in my brain. But there was still so much more to know and to learn and I functioned like a child must, when learning a language. I did my best to say what I knew and I understood as much as I could and sometimes, words and phrases pierced through the rush of sounds and I'd think–ah–now I understand that word.

It became like filling in one of those difficult one-thousand piece puzzles. Grasping one word allowed another to stick and another till suddenly a clump of words huddled together in my brain and created a space of "more French," like filling in an image in the puzzle.

After my five-day visit in Normandy, I met Maïté in Paris, where we planned to spend a night with a friend before taking the train back to Aix together. The recent storms had flooded the Seine and the river lapped along the cement quays and stairs where locals and tourists usually strolled.

The Eiffel Tower glowed with white lights and an illuminated sign that counted down the days till the new millennium. On the 28th of December, the sign read: *Jour 3*. Three days left. As we crossed the Pont Neuf Bridge, the setting sun painted the sky bright orange, pink and lavender. The river glistened silver and in the background, the lights of the Eiffel Tower twinkled: an unforgettable image of Paris during the final hours of the twentieth century.

Back in Aix, I walked from the train station to *Rue des Bernadines* and climbed the stairs to *deuxième étage, à gauche,* third floor, on the left. I had to jiggle the ancient key in the lock, just so, a little up and to the right, till I heard the click, before the old door creaked open. I peeked in, tentatively–I'd heard that apartments got broken into a lot in France, and feared that having been gone for a week, mine might have been.

But the hand-embroidered tablecloth I'd picked up at the open market for 28ff, or four dollars, still covered the weathered pine table. The tall purple iris, in a vase made from a blue juice bottle, with the label soaked off, stood in the center of the table, next to my candle.

I crept in, the cool tiles echoing my footsteps in the quiet. Dishes sat on the counter in my new, white plastic dish drainer. The air felt chilly, from no heat for a week of cold December nights and from the *mistral* winds that, at that moment, rattled the French doors and windows.

The afternoon winter sun slanted in, lighting up the golden plastered walls and the orange floor tiles. I let out the breath that I didn't know I'd been holding, moved around the corner to the bedroom, and put down my suitcase.

There was still much to do to fix it all up and make it my own. Simple lace curtains for the windows, a cover for the couch and pillows. But my bed was neatly made with the fresh new sheets and borrowed blankets.

It all felt so cozy, welcoming and comforting on that cold December afternoon, just days before the twentieth century would end and the twenty-first century would begin. With over six months left of my adventure in France, this important piece of my life was finally in place: a home of my own.

I had solitude, to write and to spend quiet time looking at my life. And just down the stairs and out the long dark hall, the vibrant energy of Aix waited, with streets full of people at any hour of the day and most hours of the night.

I wanted to pinch myself. Safe in my own apartment, I was making a life in France, finding my way. What might lie ahead in the rest of my precious time here? I was breathless to find out.

11

Le Réveillon et Le Nouveau Millennium:
New Year's Eve and The New Millennium

Through the AAGP and Maïté, I'd made a lot of new friends and was invited to a New Year's Eve/New Millennium Party at the home of two Americans, Jonathan and Holly. Everyone brought food and wine, and we all chatted and laughed, excited to be sharing this momentous occasion, many of us far from home. Just before midnight, we trooped down to the *Cours Mirabeau* to join throngs of thousands of revelers for a parade and fireworks.

At exactly midnight, the main fountain at the foot of the grand boulevard erupted in a huge fireworks display. The crowd roared. We hugged each other and shared our amazement–a new century had begun. I was thrilled to celebrate this new moment in time and history, living in France.

Back at the party, we sat in a circle and shared our New Year's resolutions. Except that these were not just New Year's resolutions, they were *New Millennium* resolutions. We Americans had to explain the concept of resolutions to our French friends. They had never heard of them and found the whole idea rather amusing.

When my turn came, I blurted out two resolutions. The first one was to go skinny-dipping in the Mediterranean. The second was to write an article about my time in France and sell it to a major New York magazine. Again, we had to explain what the term 'skinny-dipping' meant to our French friends, since there was no literal translation for that particular phrase. They laughed when they understood.

The party broke up about two in the morning. On the walk back to my apartment, with the streets still crowded with revelers, I snuggled down into my warm coat, full of the wonder of my life at that precise moment.

At ten that morning, we all met up again to take a hike and picnic up Mont Sainte Victoire, the nearby mountain represented in more than forty of Cezanne's paintings. We carpooled to the base of the mountain, then gathered again to begin our climb. Gil, a local who ran a French language school, headed up the group as we started up the trail. "On y go," he laughed, mixing up the French phrase of '*on y va*,' which means, 'let's go,' to a 'Franglaise' version, with the English word 'go' thrown in, just for good measure.

Mid-day, we reached the top of the mountain and found a shady spot near a rocky outpost where we stopped to picnic and rest. The crisp, sunny weather was perfect for our hike. Fresh baguettes, cheeses, apples, pears and strawberries, pâté and chocolate spilled out of various backpacks and were spread out for all to share.

As we gathered around, Gil pulled out a bottle of champagne and some glasses and we toasted and cheered our good fortune. I looked at my group of new friends and then out over the rolling hills and valleys towards Aix and beyond to the Mediterranean and all I could think of was, *Quelle Chance!* What luck!

We all enjoyed the day so much that we agreed to meet on other Sundays to hike again, elsewhere in the region. Two weeks later, our hike took us along the cliffs of the Mediterranean. A Scottish man and a Dutchman led the group that day, and found a secluded cove for our picnic. After we'd all shared another scrumptious array of food from our packs, the two leaders asked if anyone wanted to take a dip.

Seeing an opportunity to complete the first of my New Year's and New Millennium's resolutions, I raised my hand. "Sure, I'll do it!"

No one else wanted to test the icy water. I told the two guys about my resolution, ducked behind a rock, took off my clothes and jumped into the chilly Mediterranean. The cool, clean water felt energizing and refreshing. I could only be right there in that pure sensation. I couldn't help but hoop and holler, both from the cold and from the thrill of completing that somewhat daring resolution.

We were away from the group and I realized that the two men were not Puritans, but Europeans, used to nudity, so I sat on a rock in the sun to dry off, letting the deliciousness of the warm rays dry my skin. The Scot handed me a flask of some kind of Scottish fire water and I took a swig, then let it tingle my taste buds and down into my stomach as I turned my face up to the sun.

Ah yes, this new millennium was off to a very good start.

12

The sacred, in its various guises as holy ground, art,
or knowledge, evokes emotion and commotion.

Phil Cousineau, *The Art of Pilgrimage*

Janvier: January

I was gaining a new appreciation for just how easy it was to speak English and how fluent I was in my native tongue. In contrast, living in French, within the culture, with no subtitles, offered no way out except to do my best, open my mouth and stretch my brain, day after day.

That the words sounded musical and lyrical as they left my tongue or entered my mind, as they did in French, helped. Living there, I experienced many interesting challenges with the language that I had never encountered when I'd merely traveled in France.

Early in the New Year, I set out to get a phone and Internet connection. After waiting in various lines to find the right person, I sat down with a polite young woman at the *France Telecom* office to apply for a phone. In the course of our conversation, I learned the words for phone line, phone bill, Internet connection, late fees, repair person and installation appointment, to name a few.

As we filled out all the information on the computer, I looked over her shoulder at the square that mentioned the age of my building. *Trois cents*, three hundred, it said. Just like that. The building was twice as old as the state of California.

Within a few more days, after the repair person had visited my apartment, I had my very own phone number and Internet connection, right there, twenty-four hours a day. I called Maïté to give her the number, then Gilbert and Huguette. When I'd turn on the Internet, the sound of *whirr, blum, blum, blum* would give me chills, to know that I was just about to be connected to the whole world, to my daughters, sister and friends back home, through my laptop.

My goal was to write for at least two hours every day, so each morning, I sat in my sunny space and wrote for several hours, before heading out to shop or see friends. I continued to go to the AAGP gathering each Thursday morning and the group's other fun organized activities, outings, luncheons and parties. It was such a thrill to meet new people and be able to give them my address *and* my new phone number: *zéro quatre, quarante-deux, quatre-vingt-onze, quarante et un, vingt-deux*, 04-42-91-41-22.

Aix had an open market every day of the week. On Tuesday, Thursday and Saturday, the huge market wove through the streets down near the courthouse. That market sold not only the usual fresh produce, breads, eggs, olives and other scrumptious items, but also clothing, fabrics, tablecloths and napkins in bright Provençal prints.

One vendor set out tables of jumbled clothing and linens; at his stand, I began to discover cross-stitched tablecloths for 28ff or four dollars. I'd sort through his piles and most days would discover yet another one, usually buried at the bottom of old shirts, dresses, pants and t-shirts; it felt like a treasure hunt. Someone had patiently sewn each of those stitches onto the cotton cloth, in soft pastel colors and I was delighted to find them and to appreciate their worth. They became gifts and part of my stash of special souvenirs to take home.

At another booth at this market, I bought yards of bright Provençal fabric to make a cover for my couch, then two more contrasting fabrics for pillows. Maïté loaned me her sewing machine for that project.

I experienced such pleasure in making my apartment my own. At the *Monoprix* store, top floor, I bought *voilages,* lace curtains, and *des tringles à rideaux*, curtain rods, for my three sets of windows: kitchen, dining room and living room. I had to borrow *un tournevis*, a screwdriver and *un marteau*, a hammer, to put them up, but once up, they provided some privacy and so much beauty. On days when I opened the windows, they fluttered in the breeze.

Monoprix proved invaluable for other items: *ouvre-boîtes,* can opener, *spatule de caoutchouc,* rubber spatula, *cuillère en bois,* wooden spoon, *éplucheur à legumes,* vegetable peeler, etc., all new words added to my vocabulary. At a flea market, I bought some antique plates, bowls and wine glasses. These went up on the sideboard in my dining room. I always kept fresh flowers from the markets on my table, in my blue juice bottle, turned into a vase.

Each item made the place become more my home. I didn't think about the reality of leaving in six months. I just wanted the joy of living there day-by-day and moment-by-moment.

I was living my adventure in France without a car, which wouldn't have been possible in California, where I lived two miles from the nearest town. But living in the *centre ville* of Aix, I could reach anywhere within a half hour's walk. I loved the time being out and about on foot, immersed in my life there, able to hear the chatter of French, the church bells, to breathe in all the delicious aromas emanating from the various bakeries and restaurants, and to be a part of the day-to-day lives of the locals.

When the months of walking for hours each day had worn out my shoes, I went in search of a new pair. My Scandinavian heritage made me taller than most of the French and I soon discovered that no shoe stores in Aix carried my size. I went to them, one by one, and, after greeting the man who approached me, I would ask, *Quarante-trois?* Forty-three?

"Non, madame," each one would say, shaking his head, some in disbelief, some with a look of *horreur* that I could be so unfortunate as to have such giant feet. After visiting every possible store, I realized that my feet were simply too big for the country. At home, in America, there was no question of being able to walk into a shoe store and buy a pair of shoes, but not in Aix.

I finally solved the problem at the end of January, on a trip to Paris, where I bought hiking boots at a sporting goods store on *Boulevard St. Michel.* My winter uniform from then on consisted of my long, chic wool coat, my scarf and–*drum roll here*–hiking boots. They were very nice hiking boots, brown suede with black laces, but still, they *were* hiking boots. Luckily, none of my new friends seemed to mind, but just laughed when I told them my story, glad I'd found a solution to my need for shoes.

A similar situation happened in clothing stores. I loved French clothes and even more so when bright red *soldes*, or sales signs were plastered all over the store windows, announcing price reductions. In America, though tall, I wear an average size. In France, however, I'm considered XL. Unlike the shoe situation, however, this proved to be an advantage.

During *les soldes*, all the petite Frenchwomen would be competing for the tiny sizes and I'd waltz in, go to the XL section and pick out whatever I wanted, no pushing or shoving required. I also discovered that in the unmentionable *sous vête-ments de femme* department, I wore a size ninety-five. You had to love a country where your brassiere size was ninety-five.

On the bottom floor of *Monoprix*, I bought my yogurt, tea, soup, flour and other staples that I couldn't buy at the open markets. *Monoprix* also had an enormous cheese counter; France is famous for having three-hundred and sixty-five types of cheeses, one for every day of the year. Several times, I stood in front of the counter staring at all the cheeses, confused and intimidated. When the stern woman seemed to be tapping her foot at my indecision, I'd end up getting a slice of Swiss or Gouda, something I knew.

One day, at the checkout line at *Monoprix*, I stood next to some young girls, obviously students. They were as tall as I was! I discovered that they were from Denmark, where my grandfather was from, the one from whom we all inherited our height. We had a good little chat about being oversized in a country of petite people and I went away smiling and a bit more comfortable with myself.

The time writing each day was paying off. I sold some stories to a travel magazine about traveling by train in France and about taking the bus in Paris. I also found the quiet hours alone rich with thoughts and insights about my life and where I wanted to go in the future.

I started promoting different offerings of writing classes and coaching services, but things like that didn't seem to happen as easily in France as they did in California. While I had a few coaching clients from America, I watched my funds diminish week by week. In addition, the man with whom I'd been working for three and a half years wasn't keeping his word about paying me for the ongoing coaching clients.

The resultant stress about money brought up shame that I had carried with me for my whole life and the mean voice started talking to me. *How could you do this, get yourself here so precariously? What were you thinking? Surely you could have been more prepared!*

My challenging inner thoughts contrasted completely with the pleasurable life I was living, in French, in France. But I had to solve the money issue.

Just before I'd left California the previous November, I'd taken out a home equity loan on my farm. The bank had been sending me letters for years, showing fancy boats and cars and asking, "Why don't you use your equity to have what you really want?" I didn't want a boat or a car, but I *did* want to go to France and just in case I ran into snags earning during my eight months, I thought I'd better have a back-up plan. I didn't want to resort to it, but at this point, it was my safety net. The farm was helping me to live my dream in France.

In the meantime, I wrote a strong email standing up to the man who wasn't paying me, using all my newly found courage and strength to tell him to keep his word.

I began to see that my issues with money were just another way to dramatize 'not being enough.' If down deep I worried that I was not enough, then having not enough money fit right in there. I wanted to heal and perhaps, having to face this issue in France, could be a part of the healing. At least, that is what I was praying for.

Another interesting aspect of living alone in my sweet space and taking the time to write was that I started having dreams about my life when I was nineteen. My childhood home, being at UCLA, being with my parents; night after night, I dreamt about my earlier life, my earlier self.

I was there to explore, as Robert Frost said, "the road not taken," and who I might have been if I'd taken that road. It was as if my psyche knew that and brought up lots of deep images to support me on that journey. It was also the first time in my life that I had ever experienced stretches of unscheduled time, along with my deep intentions of self-discovery and some maturity to face what was surfacing.

Somehow, in France, the country where I felt safe and free, and within the language I so loved, I could embark on this quest and look for some answers. Answers that I hoped would not only help me to heal the past, but could allow me to create a future filled with more love and joy.

Balancing all the inner work and worry that was happening inside, in English, I could escape down the stairs and out the large, wooden creaking door to life in Aix. One cold January day, I found myself back in the central plaza and outside the teashop that I'd visited during my first few days in Aix. The sycamore trees, in France called plane trees, had since lost all their gold and orange leaves and stood stark against a dull, gray sky.

Again the teashop offered a refuge, a break from the isolation of my apartment and the sometimes harsh inner dialogue about my challenges. I relaxed into a chair, grateful for the warm murmur of French in the background and the formal manners of the waitress as she greeted me, *"Bonjour, Madame."*

I ordered one of their specialties, *chocolat chaud* or hot chocolate. It arrived on a tray in a small china coffeepot, white with pink roses and a little chip on the spout. The chocolate came out so thick and rich, it barely poured out of the narrow spout. I ordered some extra steamed milk to dilute it.

As I sat and sipped my cocoa, I became giddy with the richness. Guilt crept around the edges of my consciousness, trying to ease its way in. Surely I shouldn't be allowed to keep pouring and drinking cup after cup of such rich, liquid pleasure.

I lost all track of time, caught up in the experience of that chocolate; it coursed through my veins, energizing me. I wrote in my journal, chatted with the waitress and watched the other customers, who also were relaxing in this welcoming place, on a chilly winter day.

Hours passed. As always, in France, the waitress respected my space and privacy to sit as long as I chose. People came and went as I sat on and on. Page after page filled in my journal as I sipped the thick, chocolate stew. Those hours with my *chocolat chaud* reminded me to let go into the pleasures that France offered to me, moment by moment; in this case, the deep, rich experience of chocolate.

I finally gave up trying to finish it, paid my bill, thanked the waitress and turned to go, warm, full and satisfied.

I walked out into the late winter afternoon, pulling my scarf and thick coat close around me, my hands deep in my pockets against the cold. The chilly *mistral* wind blew an abandoned newspaper about as I headed across the square and down the windy cobblestone streets toward home.

No need for dinner that night. I wondered if I'd ever be hungry again, Just a long, hot soak in my deep bathtub, a good book and then I snuggled into bed.

13

*She was getting back to the earliest sources of gladness
she could remember.*

Willa Cather, *The Song of the Lark*

Février, La Vie en Aix: February, Life in Aix

By February, the beginning of my fourth month in France, my life in Aix began to take on a rhythm and flow. I'd had the full month of January to settle in, make my pillows and covers, hang my curtains and buy more pink and red geraniums for my balcony. My quiet writing time was balanced with plenty of hours of walking and fun with my new friends.

Living in Aix, with over thirty thousand students, I was definitely in the elder category. Most of the time my life didn't overlap much with the students, but one young man's apartment shared a wall with mine. Late at night, he loved to blast his music so loud that the ancient walls shook with the vibration of the bass beat. Many nights, unable to sleep, I'd pull on my long coat over my nightie, pad down the eight stairs that separated our apartments, knock on his door and ask him to please turn it down.

After a few times, he'd open the door, not even look at me and just say, *"Okay, je la basse."* Okay, I'm turning it down.

Our exchange taught me an interesting language lesson. I'd asked him to *"s'il vous plait, descendez la musique."* I'd learned, *descendre* as the verb meaning 'to go down' and that was all that I knew. But now I'd learned that *baisser* which means 'to lower' was the better word.

As a writer, who so loved the fine distinctions between words and the pleasure of finding the perfect one when writing in English, it was humbling to know that I was making those kinds of mistakes in French. But the other side of humbling was the pleasure of adding another new word to my vocabulary.

By this time in my stay, I also began to notice cultural differences that caused some irritation. My street, *Rue des Bernadines*, was the second to last cobblestone street of the old part of town, before the main boulevards began. I loved its location, but living day-to-day life on the edge of the *centre ville*, I discovered one major drawback.

People seemed to think that if they walked the two to three blocks to this street, that *Fifi* the poodle could do her business while the owner looked away and then they could both trot off home. *C'était fini!* All done! Then I'd walk out of my apartment and *ooh, là, là.* What a mess.

This was a problem all over Aix, with attractive, well-groomed and sensible French people, the kind who would only eat a perfectly ripe Beaufort cheese with the correct Cabernet Sauvignon. They wore expensive designer clothes and shoes and embodied all the sensibilities that we value in the French. Yet, these same folks could somehow pretend nonchalance as their dogs pooped, as if they had no responsibility whatsoever in the resultant mess and stink.

Men riding giant street cleaning machines with water streaming out and circular scouring brushes came by, almost daily, to wash the streets. But no one could seem to cajole the French to do their own individual dog duty. *Une mystère.* I was left pondering why this could be–and having to pay close attention to where I stepped.

I also discovered that, in France, pedestrians do not have the right of way. More than once, crossing the main street, *Cours Mirabeau*, it felt like a car shaved the hairs off my arms as I experienced another near miss. Like watching for dog poop, I learned to cross the street carefully and to not expect them to stop, especially when a large Mercedes barreled towards me, looking like it intended to run me over.

I was there to become fluent in French and my brain felt like a sponge, but some days that sponge refused to hold even one more tiny drop of water. If I was tired, worried, and/or lonely, it seemed as if I knew no French at all. Or my accent clashed against my own ears, and I could only imagine what it did to French ones.

Nevertheless, something stirred in this language and speaking it felt like a deep letting go, a breathing deeper and fuller. Perhaps half my soul was French, or I had an identical soul/self who lived here. Or it was past lives. Even as my brain stretched to absorb the language and nuances of this culture, it was as if I'd known it before. Which made it even harder when I struggled, *because somehow I knew this before.*

But most days were good days. I'd hear a word or phrase and 'clink,' I'd know it and begin to use it. One February afternoon, as I walked down the street towards home, I came upon a scene so entertaining, that I had to step to the side in the narrow lane and watch.

Two men were trying to maneuver a bulky, green Naugahyde couch into the second story window of an ancient building. They'd tied ropes to the couch, and one man was in the flat, trying to pull it up, while the other one, down on the street, tried to direct its movement.

But the enormous couch dwarfed the narrow window. The

guy on top kept trying to guide it in, but no matter what he did, he couldn't succeed. The couch dangled overhead and people streamed past underneath, oblivious. I, however, stood transfixed.

The petite Frenchman below jumped and reached, trying to help, but the two stories between he and the other man gaped large. The man on top was now on a ledge outside the window, gasping and pulling with all his male might. He must have really loved this couch! Some daring and exciting events must have happened on it. Or maybe it was like an old friend and represented comfort at the end of the day, where he'd sit, beer in hand, watching the télé.

At last, he got it at an angle, long-ways. crammed up against the tall window, then managed to slink in before he turned and pulled. The man below, who'd been straining in his helplessness, announced at this moment, *"j'arrive,"* I'm coming; he disappeared into the building. The two hands tugging at the large couch became four–his helper had arrived. A moment of suspense, pulling, tugging, straining, and then the couch slid into the window, out of sight.

The couch was home. I laughed out loud. What entertainment life presents and how funny we humans are. And I'd had another French lesson. *"J'arrive,"* means I'm coming. Not *je viens,* which I would have used. Another distinction between just being understood and knowing the fine points of a language.

As I continued my way along the *Rue Bedarrides,* I remembered the summer I was eight: we were going to be away so we rented our house to some foreigners. As my father explained things to the renter, I tagged along. At one point, the man asked, "How do I close the light?" I thought how silly he was, that he would say "close the light" when, of course, it should have been "turn off the light."

But now, as I struggled to learn the nuances of French, I began to see that I made mistakes like that all the time.

At *Monoprix*, when I was looking to buy something for my apartment and didn't know the word–for sponge mop, for example, *une éponge*–the saleswomen responded to my pantomimes with smiles and wide eyes. They were never condescending, aware perhaps of the effort it took to survive alone in another culture, language and city far, far from home.

Their sweetness often touched me. Something we seemed to have lost in America in our rush to achieve and to consume.

At the open market near the courthouse, an older man roasted chickens on a spit, the rich aroma of the chicken and potatoes wafting around his cart and out over the nearby olives, tapenade and loaves of freshly baked bread. He always gave me extra potatoes, the crispy, browned ones I really liked, beyond what I knew I'd paid for.

When I'd thank him, looking forward to the delicious meal I would enjoy at my table, with a glass of local white wine, he'd nod and smile. *"Je vous en prie, madame."* A very formal "you're welcome," as if I'd somehow earned this special treat in a life that was unfolding each day, including, at that particular moment, his juicy and perfectly cooked chicken and the extra scoop of crispy, browned potatoes.

Years before, when was traveling in France doing various magazine stories, I had to get to Digne-les-Bains during a rail strike. I stood in the aisle of a bus already crammed with too many bodies vying for seats and almost cried as I told the conductor, in halting French, that I had to get a seat on this bus; someone was waiting to pick me up in Digne.

Calm and patient, he turned to look at me. Touching me lightly on the sleeve, he said simply, "I'll get you to Digne, madame." I could have hugged him, but of course I didn't–that would have broken all the rules of polite French conduct. But

I knew I was safe in the midst of the chaos of the train strike. And that yes, he would get me to Digne.

I don't remember how he found me a seat, but when the bus let me off at the dark and deserted train station near Digne, another man in the station called a taxi to take me the rest of the way. I arrived, three hours late, but I arrived. I don't know who paid for that taxi; I didn't. It was as if unseen hands guided my way.

Maybe it's being *une femme d'un certain âge*, a woman of a certain age, as they say, traveling alone. Maybe it is because I have moments of good clear French mixed in with my strong, unforgiving American accent, especially when I am stressed or tired. Or maybe I've been just lucky. But I have been lost in the metro, gotten on the wrong train, been disoriented in the streets of Paris, vulnerable and sometimes afraid, and the French, even the Parisians, have rescued me with graciousness and respect.

I've heard that they have a 'good Samaritan' rule: if someone is in trouble, you must help them. Maybe that's it. I just know that I've found it comforting, encouraging and even moving to experience it countless times. And living in Aix, this courtesy and kindness wove through the hours and days of my life like a rich yellow thread, soothing, calming and nourishing.

14

Every journey can be sacred, soulful and transformative
if it is undertaken with a desire for risk and renewal.
Phil Cousineau, *The Art of Pilgrimage*

La Vie en Provence et Le Spa:
Life in Provence and The Spa

The Romans founded Aix-en-Provence over two thousand years ago, choosing the location because of the abundance of springs and the healing qualities of the water. The spa in Aix, *Spa Thermes Sextius,* is built on the site of the original Roman baths, utilizing a spring that bubbles up from a depth of eighty meters, at a temperature of ninety-seven degrees.

The pure water, which is used in the spa treatments, is rich in calcium, magnesium, lithium and other minerals. The spring and the crumbling walls of the ancient Roman buildings are visible through a glass floor in the entry of the spa.

There is a soft, almost cocoon-like quality to French hydrotherapy spas. Maybe it is because we all started our lives floating in warm water, or that our bodies are over sixty-percent water, but the spa experience there feels healing, comforting and renewing.

The treatments, called *soins*–which translates as 'care'–use the natural and vibrant spring water and are said to be helpful in relieving stress, fatigue and even cellulite. The spa experience is designed to give you a sense of being *bien dans votre peau*, good in your skin. It's all about pleasure and relaxation. Even the soft murmur of French in the background helps you to let go.

I first discovered the sensuous world of French hydrotherapy spas in 1994, on a trip with my then nineteen-year-old daughter, Heather. We arrived in Normandy, both stressed out: me from work and Heather from college finals. At this spa, they used the Atlantic seawater for their treatments.

We slipped into the nurturing space of the spas as easily as we slipped into its bubbling warm water. We spent idyllic days padding around in thick terry cloth robes and rubber slippers being *soignée*–cared for by the attentive staff.

We were painted with warm algae or mud and wrapped up to rest. Or massaged while warm water showered down on us. Or settled into a *bain hydromassant*, bubbling baths with essential oils and jets that massaged us from head to toe.

The natural and vibrant water was full of life force and minerals. We recovered from our jet lag. We got rid of toxins; we filled up with energy and well-being. I felt better than I had in years.

"This is sooo cool, Mom," Heather said. I agreed. I also began to wonder: was this one of the secrets of the French for staying slim and beautiful?

So I was thrilled to find out that Aix had its very own spa, just a five-minute walk from my apartment. It not only offered the wonderful *soins* with the source water and local mineral-filled mud, but a reasonable rate for locals to buy a *forfeit*–a package of treatments. My forfeit also entitled me to use the pool, Jacuzzi, steam, sauna and exercise room for the day.

So my life in February took on an easy rhythm. I'd write in the morning, then head out to meet Maïté or other friends for tea or lunch, go to the open market or stop by the American University library for some books. Once a week, I'd go to the spa. Each time, I'd marvel at my good fortune and remind myself to enjoy every precious moment of the luxury.

At the open markets, I could choose from a dazzling array of fresh foods sold by local farmers. Bright red, juicy strawberries, crunchy apples, sweet carrots and a bright green head of lettuce so large it looked like I was stuffing a green wig into a plastic bag. Brown eggs, feathers still stuck to them from the Provençal hen who'd laid them that morning, rested in a wicker basket; I could count out how many I wanted, place them into a partial egg carton, and tuck them into my straw shopping bag. Bananas and some other produce came from Sierra Leone in Africa, reminding me just how far away from California I was.

On a previous trip to France, shopping at an open market during the summer, I was choosing a melon and the farmer asked, "*Pour aujourd'hui or pour demain?*" For today, or for tomorrow? He then chose the one perfect for that day, not the one that would be perfect for tomorrow, teaching me a new respect for the art of choosing melons.

I'd finally learned to walk more slowly, stroll even, as I lived my life on foot, in Aix. What was the rush, after all? I had time, a first in my life. I'd sit at my favorite outdoor café in the central plaza, sipping a *grande crème décafféinée*, savoring the combination of both bitter and sweet tastes, with the lump of brown sugar I'd stirred into the cup.

The winter sun filtered through the bare plane trees and warmed me, as I wrote in my journal with my favorite new fountain pen. As I listened to the sound of the water flowing in the nearby fountain, I marveled that I was sitting in the plaza where I'd first known that Aix was where I needed to come to live.

I'd wave at babies, missing my grandbaby, breathe in the aroma of croissants from a nearby bakery and drink in the experience of relaxing, surrounded by the musical sounds of French.

Becoming a mother when I'd just turned twenty, I'd never had much free time. But now, with my group of international friends, we'd spend long afternoons at a café, comparing our experiences of life in France in a combination of French and English, then head to a movie or dinner. I'd never been so care-free in my life.

I could sense a new me emerging, and I liked her. When I looked in the mirror, the face that looked back at me seemed relaxed, happy. She had blond streaks and a chic haircut and wore fashionable clothes bought at *les soldes* at *Etam*, the reasonably priced store with the latest French styles. It was as if my nineteen- year-old self fueled me with her energy and vitality. I'd come to rescue her and now she was rescuing me.

I sensed new strength and confidence and, even at fifty-one, more maturity. Living in France, living abroad for almost a year, was a piece of my education that I'd always wanted to have. A part of me was growing up, and an aspect that hadn't come forward in time, now filled her place in the fabric of my life.

The AAGP organized lots of interesting outings to explore the area around Aix and one of them took us to an estate on the Mediterranean, about a half hour away. We toured the extensive gardens and buildings that bordered the sparkling blue sea.

As I stood on the terrace, looking out at the water, the warm winter sun and the bright yellow mimosa flowers reminded me of the Southern California of my youth, peaceful, uncrowded and unspoiled. I relished it all, especially the mystery of being so at home in this place that was also new to me.

I'd brought my bathing suit, hoping to have another chance for a refreshing dip into the sea and after we lunched at a nearby café, I saw my chance and jumped in. How had I ended up so blessed as to be swimming in the Mediterranean on a February day, in Provence? I put my head back into the cool water, closed my eyes and said to the sky, *thank you, thank you, thank you.*

The well-known American food writer, Patricia Wells, who lived in Paris and Provence, had been the speaker at our January AAGP meeting. The room was packed and after her presentation, I introduced myself as a free-lance writer. She invited me to come and spend a day in one of her cooking classes at her home in Provence, in the village of Vaison La Romaine.

So early on a bright mid-February day, I borrowed Maïté's car for the four-hour drive north. I stepped out of the car at precisely 10:00 am, and took in the huge oak tree sheltering the outdoor table, the view looking out onto the vineyards and olive trees, and the stillness.

In her sunny kitchen, Patricia greeted me warmly, then handed me a crisp apron and I joined the group of students who were gathered around preparing food on her various counters.

We worked together all morning, slicing and sautéing, sifting and folding to create a four-course lunch that featured local truffles, called 'black gold,' due to their high price tag. Their potent, *sauvage* flavor imbued soup, salad, main course and even our dessert. After we shared that delicious repast in her dining room, with local wines paired to each dish, we headed out on a truffle hunt with a local farmer.

Puffy white clouds scuttled across the winter sky, blown by gusts of the chilly mistral, as we trudged through a sparse grove of oak trees behind the farmer and his dog. (One time when my hiking boots came in handy.) The dog trotted ahead, then, smelling a truffle, stopped, whined, and pawed the ground. The stocky, ruddy farmer dug it out, then rewarded the pooch with a tiny piece of sausage. The truffles smelled pungent and earthy, rich and musky. It began to rain lightly as we followed the farmer and dog in this age-old hunt for the treasured truffles.

After visiting a truffle processing plant, the group returned to Patricia's home, and I headed back to Aix, full of gratitude for being included in the rich, full day. I'd discovered, prepared and eaten my first, 'black gold.'

Towards the end of February, standing at my stove, stirring a packet of soup, I was reading the directions as I went along. I realized that I didn't know all the words on the package, but I *understood* what they meant. Recognizing that as a huge milestone, I jumped around my kitchen, waving the wooden spoon in my hand, triumphant.

Soon after that, I was having lunch at Maïté's and as everyone chattered in rapid French, I realized I could understand and respond, without thinking. Maïté noticed and congratulated me on my new proficiency and confidence in the language. I called Gilbert and Huguette often, chatting easily, never getting over the thrill of our being in the same country and time zone.

15

La Visite de Ma Mère: My Mother's Visit

M y mother and sister Sharon were scheduled to come and
visit me for three weeks at the end of February. I dreaded having my mother visit. In my fifty-one years, we'd never
been able to find a way to interact without her being cold and
critical and me reacting defensively.

Four years before, when I'd taken her to France to meet
Gilbert, the fact that I spoke the language and she didn't made
her dependent on me. While that experience hadn't exactly improved our relationship, it had at least shifted the balance of it
a bit. Maybe that would work in my favor on this trip too.

My sister Sharon, on the other hand, was kind and caring.
But it seemed that she had new lesions in her brain and might
not be able to come. Lots of emails flew back and forth trying
to sort it all out. In the end, they ended up coming separately,
for three weeks each. They did not consult me about this, nor
ask if it would be all right that I was to have one guest after
another in my apartment for six weeks, instead of two guests
together for three weeks.

Their coming separately also meant that I would be alone
with my mother, without the loving buffer of my sister, and
that worried me. I hoped that the new strength and sense of
self that I had discovered in my four months in France could

withstand the harsh and critical reality of my mother.

As a result of many therapy sessions and personal growth seminars, I'd managed to piece together an explanation for the challenges I faced with my mother. Her father had deserted the family when she was a toddler, just before her sister was born. So she'd grown up without a father, hated her younger sister, and distrusted men.

I came along, the last of four children, and adored my dad, who was loving and warm. Mom was jealous of my closeness with my father. For as far back as I could remember, she treated me with coldness and anger and, when I was younger, with physical abuse. I was also 'the younger sister,'–my sister Sharon being two years older–and Mom seemed to be living out her resentment of her own sister with me.

I'd spent my whole adult life trying to heal the wounds from our relationship. In our interactions, we managed to superficially get along, sort of tolerate each other, but with no deep caring or emotion expressed. Being with her alone would be a real test that I hoped I could pass.

The last week in February, I again borrowed Maïté's car, to pick up my mother from the Marseille airport. In spite of my nervousness, she was my first official visitor, and I was excited to share my life in Aix with her. I'd decided to give her my bedroom; I'd sleep on the *click-clack* couch in the living room.

She seemed to like my apartment, but Mom was not one to give out many compliments. The first day, we walked to the spa, to set her up to go for a series of treatments. She'd experienced the French spas on a previous trip in Normandy and not only loved the treatments, but the attention she received for her age. I taught her how to say *quatre-vingt-quatre*, eighty-four, to announce her age. Of course, they'd never ask, but she wanted them to know.

The walk to the spa wasn't long, just two blocks down *Rue des Bernadines*, then a right turn and two long blocks down *Cours Sextius* to the end of the street. We'd walked it together twice, so on the first day of her treatments, Mom was able to manage it by herself. As I watched her walk away, some guilt seeped in for sending her off on her own, but I so needed that time to myself.

She walked stooped over and wobbled a bit on the cobblestones, but made it to the right turn on *Cours Sextius*, then disappeared out of sight. It reminded me of watching my children walk away towards school all those years ago, that sense of wanting to protect them and hoping that they would be okay. But those hours alone helped me to not only try to get some writing done but also to fortify myself for the intense experience of being with her.

Maïté helped me to entertain her with excursions, shopping and lunches. We drove to the nearby perched village of Gordes, empty of tourists in February and enjoyed lunch in a café on the central plaza there, looking out over the fields of Provence.

Except for negotiating the cobblestones, Mom walked well. On one of our trips around Aix, we happened into *St. Jean de Malte*, the 13th century church where two months before I'd sung Christmas carols in English. That afternoon, candlelight flickered on the golden walls and the fragrance of incense lingered from an earlier service.

As we sat down to rest in the cool, quiet space, the calm and comfort of the holy place enveloped me and I vowed to return on my own. I noticed in the bulletin that the church offered three services a day led by monks, *matins, mass et vespers*, morning prayers, mass and evening prayers.

Most days, Mom and I ate lunch out and cooked dinner at my place at night. Next to my favorite bakery, there was *une boucherie*, a butcher's shop, where we lined up with the other patrons to pick out our choices of meat. The veal, beef and chicken we cooked tasted fresh and delicious, with the herbs, salad and vegetables we bought at the open market.

Mom wanted to drive to the Cote d'Azur, Nice and Cannes, so I arranged to rent a car and set up an itinerary for the trip. I had a long-time friend, Nicole, who I'd met when our daughters were small and she was visiting San Francisco as a medical resident. Nicole and her husband were radiologists in Nice and invited us to stay with them during our visit.

Early March proved to be a perfect time to visit Nice; the day were fresh and crisp and there were no crowds. We lunched on the beach in Cannes, a place that would be swamped with tourists in the summer. As we sat and enjoyed our fresh seafood salad with a glass of white wine, waves lapping just a few feet away, we marveled at the peaceful scene. Mom seemed to be having fun; the excitement of France smoothed things out a bit between us and we were doing pretty well.

One of Nicole's brothers spoke English, which meant that Mom had someone to chat with amid all the French. He told us about a place in the Alps with hot springs, and I made a note of that, as Sharon wanted to visit the Alps on her trip. After exploring the Roman ruins and the Matisse museum and relaxing at Nicole's lovely home, we headed back towards Aix.

A friend had recommended a hotel called *Bormes Les Mimosas* in the little village of Lavandou, along the route back. After checking in, Mom and I sat on our tiny balcony looking out over the Mediterranean and drank a toast of champagne. I remembered that this was the village where Willa Cather had written her famous quote about happiness. Taking in the peaceful scene, I could see why.

Mom was getting a wonderful tour with me planning, driving, tour guiding and interpreting. Though she didn't come out and thank me, she seemed pleased and happy, so I was relieved. The woman at the hotel told me that I spoke French perfectly with an *"accent charmant."* I was pleased, sensing the progress that four months living in France had provided, not only in my sense of confidence in general, but in my fluency in French.

Back in Aix, we had another five days before Mom left. I was reluctant to tell her about my financial stresses, since that would provoke a lecture about "how I hadn't used my potential" and "when was I going to get a real job." That, of course, would overlook the fact that if I had a "real job," we wouldn't be sitting together in my apartment in France. But logic like that never seemed to interfere with my mother's judgments.

Sometimes it felt like there was an imaginary daughter, who looked like me and had my abilities, but lived a fantasy life that my mother thought that I was supposed to be living. It didn't matter that the fantasy life did not represent my choices or aspirations. This phantom daughter was perfect, and I was not, and my mother thought it was her duty to continually point that out to me.

The fantasy daughter would be rich by now. It wasn't cool that I was not. My sister Sharon was not rich either, but she had always gotten a pass with my mother. Luckily Sharon and I loved each other, in spite of the difference in our relationships with our mother.

Having my mom there not only took over my personal space, it also put a strain on my budget. I was not able to write much while she was there, nor could I do any coaching or lead writing groups. We also ate lunch out most days and she insisted on always splitting the bill.

When I finally spoke up and asked if she would be willing to chip in on the rent, since she was staying for three weeks, she offered me $100, less than a fifth of my rent. When I then told her that I thought she should help out more, she handed over another $100 but then gave me her cold, hard glare, followed by the silent treatment and a retreat to my bedroom with her crossword puzzle.

On one of her last nights in Aix, we sat at my table sipping wine after dinner. A car honked in the narrow street below and the curtain fluttered at the open window. We'd spent the day shopping for mom to buy things for herself and friends at home and I was tired. For some reason, the conversation turned to her relationship with my father.

She waved her wineglass at me and then set it down, glaring at me as she announced that I had caused her divorce with my father.

Both shocked and outraged, I sat up straight in my chair.

"I did *not* cause your divorce. You and my father were *adults*. You were unhappy my whole childhood and I was seventeen years old when you split up! If you got a divorce, that was your choice. How dare you blame that on *me*. It was not my fault."

And with that last statement, I pounded my fist on my old pine table with all the force I had. The wine glasses teetered. I wondered later if the student who shared a wall with me could feel the building shake or if people out on the street could hear my yelling, but I did not care. I shocked both of us with my fury. It felt so good to let it out.

I had to give her credit. She didn't flinch. She just sat there. I was crying by then, overcome by the pain of all the years of misunderstanding with this woman, my mother. Was this why she had always been cold and critical to me? Because she blamed me for her divorce?

I had never before stood up to my mother, nor had we ever had such a straightforward conversation In spite of her blaming me for something she imagined I'd done, at least we were actually addressing it. And my outburst shifted things in the invisible space between us. I had said, *No, I will not be treated like that. I deserve better.*

I was reminded of the scene in *Oliver Twist* when hungry little Oliver says, "Please sir, I want some more." With my mother, I had always felt, "Please, I want some more," starved for her love and affection, always hoping for more. But the scene at the table began to change things.

I brought up how, in my childhood, she'd taken my sister and me along when she'd gone to visit another man in Los Angeles.

"How could you *do* that? We were ten and twelve."

She denied that it had been an affair, claiming that he was just a friend.

"But you walked with him arm and arm. You looked into his eyes, danced with him, let him take us out to dinner and a movie. People thought we were a *family*. But all the while, Dad was home alone. How could you *do* that?"

She couldn't answer my questions. I knew that. But if felt so good to finally ask them, to let out all the confusion I'd carried for all those years. To see, once again, that the woman who sat across from me was not perfect. Was that why she wanted me to be? Because she had failed in so many ways to be perfect herself?

We were still the same mother and daughter, with a long history of pain, but something had shifted. We had said what had been unsayable and to some degree it cleared the air. I had broken out of the invisible rules of who I had to be, especially with my mother. What if those rules were gone and I was free? Free to express my feelings, ask for what I wanted and needed, free to tell the truth?

Later that evening, we hugged each other and I cried again, saying that I hoped that somehow we could be closer. She hugged me back, her pajamas soft against my face, and her familiar smell comforting. What if this time in France could heal all of my childhood demons, letting them out to fly away? What if my tears had softened the hard ground between us, allowing her to soften too?

Two days later, we left the apartment before dawn to get her to the airport. I sent her off into Air France, gate 41, with a box of fruit and yogurt in her bag, like sending a child off with a school lunch. She looked small and fragile with her white hair, as she disappeared into the crowd. She didn't look back.

As I watched her, I saw how soon, in my lifetime, she would disappear to the other side of life and not be there anymore. Tears welled up at that, and I wiped them away as I watched the plane back up and taxi down the runway, then lift out of sight.

After returning Maïté's car, I went back to bed and slept till noon. That night, still exhausted, I slept for fourteen hours. I had two days on my own before my sister arrived for three weeks.

I was reminded of the book, *A Year in Provence*, and how dangerous it was proving to be to have an apartment in Provence, where people thought they were entitled to come and stay.

16

Something soft and wild and free,
something that whispered to the ear on the pillow,
lightened the heart, softly, softly picked the lock,
slid the bolts, and released the prisoned spirit of man
into the wind…
Willa Cather, *Death Comes for the Archbishop*

Mars: March

In the three weeks of my mother's visit, I had missed the time alone to write and think and wander the streets of Aix, in my cocoon of learning and healing. With all my mother's demands, I was afraid that I might have lost some of the fragile new spaces I'd so recently discovered.

But when I sat down again on my couch with the cover and the pillows I'd sewn, in the quiet space of my apartment, with the morning sunlight streaming in, I could sense the ground that I had taken.

I wrote in my journal,

This new closeness, with my self, with my soul, feels delicate.
Like a sense of the mystery and the magic of life. I was afraid I'd
lost sight of it, but now can know that it is always there.

So far, my life has been mostly about trying to heal. Now
I want to be healed and say, Good. Healed. Let's go from here.

The inner journey is the most important and yet we live in a culture that barely acknowledges it. Outer, outer, outer. Body, car, house, the shell. What about your soul? It's 10 pm. Do you know where your soul is?

I could see the healing that had begun with my mother. Not a complete transformation, but progress nonetheless. That healing was appropriate for my nineteen-year-old self, too; I now understood, looking back, that one of the reasons I'd rushed headlong into marriage and motherhood had been to escape from my mother.

I took those two days before my sister arrived to relish my freedom, sleep in my own bed again, write as much as possible and prepare for my next visitor. That included a trip to *la Laverie*, the Laundromat on the corner, to wash the sheets and towels.

I was still struggling with my former business partner to get him to pay me what he owed me. After the time with my mother, I was able to see that I had a pattern of creating unfulfilling relationships, in which I was not respected, taken care of, or validated.

He also was selfish and self-centered, refusing to acknowledge the contribution I'd made to him in the three plus years we had worked together, by keeping his word on our agreement. I kept writing letters, which he said that he wouldn't read, but I sent them anyway. Though I felt helpless being so far away, I knew that I was entitled to the money I had earned from the work that I had done.

While painful, seeing how much that relationship resembled the one with my mother, made me determined to be more careful in the future. I needed to heal the place in me that kept generating destructive, non-supportive relationships.

I had changed from living in France. I now knew I deserved better. That same inner fire that had allowed me to pound on the table with my mother was energizing me to create a new life, without the heavy burden I'd been carrying of not being worthy, of not being enough.

One of the spiritual books I was reading said, "There's no failure, only giving up." I would not give up. My journal at that time had the phrase, *Don't forget your dreams*, decorating every few pages. As I'd see those words in my daily writing, I'd stop and think, Yes, dreams are so important. Thank you, universe, that I am able to live this one, right now.

And each morning, at the top of my page, I'd write my three special words, *"Croyez-en-soi."*

I had just passed the halfway point in my time in France. The four and a half months had been rich with growth and learning. Early on, I'd had some nights when I'd ached with loneliness, but those were behind me now. Most days, I felt energized, alive and excited. The time in Aix was turning out to be more than I could have hoped for. I wrote,

> *As I am living the reality of fulfilling my long held desire, as it is turning out, I am faced with a different challenge. What if dreams __do__ come true? Then what? Then all the cynicism of life, of the times I've turned away from myself, those were the big losses, the big mistakes.*
>
> *And this is the magic. It feels like I've turned and faced the destiny that wants to come to me, like turning to face the sun. I want to stand in this new space and to let the rest go.*

As an undergraduate at UCLA, I had studied Cultural Anthropology, where we discussed questions such as, "Who are we, as humans, beyond the influences of our cultures?" I had always wanted to have the experience of looking back at America from afar, to get a perspective on my cultural heritage. I could now see that my ancestors, on both sides of my family, had left the old world to risk going across the ocean to the new one.

On my dad's side, Scandinavian farmers left Norway and Denmark to settle in South Dakota. On my mother's side, her ancestors left Ireland and Canada to venture to the unknown place 'down under' called Australia, to begin their new lives. Then my mother came to America, met and married my father and left Australia behind.

I had it in my genes, in my DNA, to be from the new world, and I had their sense of risk and adventure in my blood. But for these eight months, I had gone back the other way, from the new world to the old world, which was giving me a perspective on what they had left behind. I'd needed to come to France and experience the 'before' of the old world.

What was it that my ancestors left behind? Established, formal and more elegant manners, for starters. In Aix, even a four-year-old boy on the street said, *"Oh, pardon,"* when he darted in front of me. Then there was the way you started out a friendship or conversation with a stranger using *vous*, the more formal version of 'you.'

After some time with that friend, you switched to *tu*, the more familiar form of 'you.' That *tu* indicated that something subtle had shifted: you'd moved to a new space in your friendship. Maïté and I'd gone through that shift quickly, after just a few visits; she'd felt like an old friend from the start.

The realtor to whom I paid my rent each month, however, remained a *vous*. Shopkeepers always addressed me as *vous*. On the other hand, one always addressed children as *tu*, which seemed to show a tender, caring view of them, which we all shared, even if we weren't related.

In my favorite neighborhood bakery, we exchanged a formal greeting as I entered–*Bonjour madame*–and an acknowledgment as we completed our little transaction: *Merci,*

Au revoir, bonsoir, they would say, with just that extra second taken to let it land, before turning to the next person in line. These could be seen as little things, but they mattered and I noticed and appreciated them.

I savored the slower lifestyle and the part that quality food and wine played in it. On Sunday mornings, bakeries would be open, with their freshly made, delectable creations–little works of art filling the windows. I'd choose a fruit tart: a tiny layer of custard topped with strawberries, kiwis, blueberries and raspberries covered with a light glaze, all of it nestled in a crisp crust, almost too beautiful to eat.

The *Place de la Mairie* had an open market on Sunday mornings, and *Monoprix* would be open for the morning hours, too. Patrons could buy all they needed for their Sunday meals, then everything closed down by mid-day.

Sunday afternoons, families strolled down *Cours Mirabeau,* pushing giant prams and holding onto toddler's hands, then sat for a long and luxuriant meal, before continuing on home. Children sat quietly and participated with the adults, which sometimes included *la grand mère et le grand père.*

Then there was art, music and culture. Aix had an excellent museum, Le Musée Granet, which showcased many of Cezanne's paintings and other treasures. I'd attended several concerts in the cathedral, sitting spellbound as Vivaldi and Beethoven echoed off the walls and out into the night air.

I relished it all, maybe because I knew how precious it was and how different from my normal life. Yet I could also appreciate what the new world represented. We were the risk takers, open to new ideas and freer in our self-expression.

A woman I'd met told me that her daughter had visited America and now carried *la rève Américaine,* the American dream. She whispered the words. It was clear she was afraid that she had lost her daughter to the new world, that somehow the old world would not satisfy her anymore.

America had huge, wild, open and untamed spaces that supported our sometimes big and wild ideas. In America, anyone could make it, with hard work and a bit of luck. I could feel both in me: my love of the new and the old worlds. And gratitude: spending this time in France, touching base with my 'old world' European roots, was nurturing me in a vital way.

Just as I was discovering a new way of being by living inside the French language, I was discovering new, soft, ancient places inside myself as I lived my day-to-day life in France.

17

*Sisters share childhood memories
and grown up dreams.*
Author unknown

Ma Soeur Sharon: My Sister Sharon

My sister and I had grown up as best friends, close and in-
separable. Then, after our parents divorced, when I was
seventeen and she was nineteen, we started fighting. During
those years, I watched my mother and her sister not speak to
each other at their own mother's funeral. That was our model;
Sharon and I were headed down that road. But I vowed that we
would not end up like that.

Sharon and I both became counselors and were involved
in personal growth courses, which motivated us to heal our
differences. Finally, in 1990, I figured out that we'd taken op-
posite sides in the divorce: I'd taken Dad's side and she'd taken
Mom's. That was one of the last pieces that we needed to sort
out, before we could reclaim the love and closeness that we'd
shared all those years before.

I decided to move to the small town in the Northern California mountains, where Sharon and her family lived. At the
time, my eldest daughter, Michelle was in college close by, and

my youngest, Heather, was in high school and living with her dad. Heather spent summers and vacations with me, and both daughters delighted in spending time with my sister's family. Sharon's three children were twelve, nine and five. We'd hike to the river or lakes in the summer, pick blackberries and make pies, and in winter go cross-country skiing.

Sharon and I had four years of fun together, jogging on chilly mornings, our breath coming out in little clouds as we chatted and laughed our way through two miles. We baked and cooked for our families, celebrated birthdays and holidays together, and shared many precious times as our lives overlapped for the first time since we'd been teenagers.

But in 1994, Sharon was diagnosed with brain tumors. In the five years since then, she had gone through two brain surgeries, chemotherapy and radiation, but nothing seemed to be able to stop the growth of the tumors in her brain. Though she'd been stable when I left in November, from the many emails that had flown back and forth, I knew that she had new lesions in a different area of her brain.

My sister had a master's degree in linguistics and, in addition to French, had learned Spanish and Swedish when she lived in Europe for two years after graduating from college. But the tumors made her seem a little off, a tiny bit disoriented. Sometimes her speech was slow, her reactions just a few seconds late, and her sense of time had definitely disappeared.

Sharon was just twenty-two months older than I, though I was taller and had bigger feet, a detail that my mother loved to point out. Sharon and I had passed for twins many times, and watching her body fail felt like watching myself deteriorate in front of my own eyes. She was my best friend and my closest ally, the person who knew everything about me and loved me anyway, my caring and kind sister, who had a huge heart.

My time in France was giving me a break from having to

deal with Sharon's almost-daily challenges. Her husband had left her two years before, and Sharon could no longer drive. So in California, I drove her to her cancer support group and to doctor's appointments, sometimes hours away. I made sure that her son got picked up when needed, and ran other errands, for groceries, prescriptions, and whatever else she might need.

When I returned, I would need to step back into my helping role. I adored my sister and wanted to support her, but had so enjoyed my break from the daily responsibility of looking out for her.

After two days of rest and solitude following my mother's departure, I stood again at the airport gate, watching the crowd for Sharon to appear.

From various emails, I knew she'd lost her passport and I wasn't sure how she'd handled that problem. At home, I would have made all her reservations and helped her pack, and wondered why she'd flown into Marseilles from Italy on Air Italia. As all the passengers from her flight walked by, I began to get concerned. Had she missed her flight? Then she appeared, wobbling a little as she walked towards me.

"Diane! There you are!" She sounded almost surprised to see me, making me worry about how much space in her brain those new lesions had taken over.

But she hugged me hard and it was so good to see her again and to feel her sweet presence. We found her overstuffed bag, which had burst open and had been fixed shut with bright yellow tape, and set off for Maïté's car in the parking lot.

The first day, as we walked around Aix, we stopped in at the *Église St. Jean de Malte* just as they were saying vespers. We sat together in the wooden pew, following along with the prayers, which were sung by the monks and the people attending. I felt the same wonderful calm that I'd felt in the church the day

Mom and I had stopped in. Sharon felt it too.

"Let's come back every day," she said and I agreed, thinking that with the three services, we could try to make it to at least one. She needed prayers and all the help we could find to heal her brain.

Sharon loved everything about Aix, my apartment, the church, the fountains, my friends, the spa. As I had with Mom, I got her set up with a series of treatments at the spa and went with her the first few times, just to make sure she knew the route. After that, she walked the short distance alone.

While she was gone, I'd hurry to write and catch up on what I needed to do. And even though we'd walked the route together, she always got lost coming back. But just when I'd start to worry about her, she'd buzz for me to let her into the building, shuffle up the three flights of stairs, and knock on the door.

I gave Sharon my bedroom and moved again into the living room. We'd cook our breakfasts, then pick up something wonderful for lunch or dinner. I borrowed Maïté's car to drive her to the perched village of Gordes and to the famous source of the Sorgue River, la Fontaine de Vaucluse. She appreciated all of it and marveled at the life I'd created in Aix. Unlike my mother, Sharon offered to help out with the rent for the time she was there.

"Of course. You're my hotel and you're taking care of me for three weeks," she said as she handed over three hundred dollars. I was grateful for her generosity.

One of the reasons I savored my time in Aix was that I knew I would be returning home to what would be the last years of my sister's life. Even at that moment, the clock was ticking. *How much time did we have left?* This would be Sharon's last visit to France.

Sharon had her heart set on going to the nearby Alps. I so wanted to be able to grant that wish, and I'd even made a reservation at a hotel in the little village of Monêtier les Bains, a ski area with natural hot springs. Maïté had again offered to loan me her car for the five-hour drive, but I was dreading driving that tiny red car on windy, icy mountain roads. I was torn, wanting to give Sharon the trip she longed for, knowing it was her last chance, but dreading the driving.

The day before we were to leave, I took a walk by myself, trying to clear my head. I had to get Sharon to the Alps, but I didn't want to drive–what could I do? My walk took me past the train station, and on a hunch, I stopped in. It turned out that there was a train to the town of Briançon, where we would be met by a bus to take us to the village up the hill.

Because we were traveling on a Tuesday, we got an amazing deal. I bought the tickets and almost skipped home to tell Sharon. We could both get what we wanted. She would get her trip to the Alps and I wouldn't have to drive.

I called Maïté to thank her and to tell her that we wouldn't need the car after all. The next morning, I ran out to gather a picnic lunch for us to take on the train: cheese, a fresh baguette, apples and berries, a half bottle of wine, and a tart for each of us. Then Sharon and I walked to the station to catch the train.

After leaving Aix, the train traveled through farmlands that stretched out in all directions, with rows of fruit trees covered in white and pink blossoms. The route followed the Durance River, past fields of lavender, which in summer would be bright with purple flowers.

Further on, the scenery became more rugged, with the craggy peaks of the Alps surrounding hamlets tucked into the mountainsides. Instead of having to focus on the road and maps, I sat across from Sharon as we enjoyed the scenery, sipped the wine with our picnic lunch, read and relaxed.

After lunch, a late spring snowstorm turned everything white with its fluffy, fat flakes. I was thrilled to be watching it all from inside the train as we chugged along. I went to the dining car and brought us each back a steaming cup of hot cocoa. We chatted and laughed, so happy to be sharing such an adventure.

At the train station in Briançon, the connecting bus stood waiting, its windshield wipers swishing back and forth against the snow and its heater warm and welcoming, to take us up the steep, snowy road to the village of Monêtier-les Bains. Once there, we walked a block to our hotel, our rolling bags making tracks in the fresh snow.

The village and our hotel both looked like something out of the children's book, *Heidi*: a wooden chalet with a crackling fire set against the backdrop of the mountains. We enjoyed a simple and delicious chicken dinner as the snow continued to pile up outside the hotel's dining room window.

Sharon loved snow and the spring storm delighted her. The next morning dawned bright and sunny, the snow glistening and sparkling like glitter. After breakfast, we set off to explore the local hot springs. For hours, we soaked in large hot pools, facing huge picture windows that looked out onto mountains and sky.

We walked, lunched, napped, then went back and soaked again before dinner. That night, the hotel put on a special spread of regional foods: rich cheese *fondue* and *raclette,* a dish consisting of melted cheese that is *raclé*, or scraped off onto bread. An oom-pah band playing polka music in the background completed the scene. The next day, after another long soak in the hot springs, we caught the bus down the hill, and the train back home to Aix.

I was thrilled that Sharon had been able to fulfill her wish to go to the Alps, and so happy that I had been able to enjoy the trip too. For those three days, it had felt like we were kids again, carefree and having fun, even with someone else in charge of moving us through space.

During the rest of Sharon's stay, we visited the church many times for one of the three services, which we both found healing and nurturing. As we sat together in the ancient church, it felt like the best of our Catholic upbringing, the incense, the mystery and the reverence, without the guilt and sin lectures that had spoiled the whole experience for both of us.

Sharon appreciated the rich subtleties of life in Aix: the open markets, the bakeries, the slower pace of life. She loved my sunny apartment and especially my big old bathtub; she didn't have one in her tiny apartment in California.

As hard as it had been to have constant visitors for six weeks, I could see that it had been perfect that my mother and sister had come separately.

For those three weeks, Sharon and I could let the magic of France distract us from the terrifying reality of what was happening inside her brain. We could just be two sisters who loved each other, sharing a delightful time.

18

*I believe that the strongest need of your nature
is to find yourself, to emerge as yourself.*
Willa Cather, *The Song of the Lark*

Avril, Le Printemps: April, Springtime

Spring arrived in Provence. The trees along *Cours Mirabeau* and around the central plaza sprouted bright new leaves and the fruit trees around town vied with each other to show off their bright pink and white blossoms. After I said goodbye to Sharon, I had almost three weeks until my next visitor. I reclaimed my bedroom, savored the time again to write and continued to visit the church where the monks sang the mass in Gregorian chants.

Heather had returned to California to help Michelle with her baby, Ellie, and I received many adorable photos of mother, auntie and baby through the Internet. Those images made me wish that I could crawl through the computer screen and hold them all in my arms, but I couldn't. I took my laptop to a place where I could print out the photos and then put them up in my apartment. Michelle and her husband Claude were coming with Ellie in May and I looked forward to seeing them and to holding my sweet grandbaby again.

There had been moments when I had considered trying to stay in France, seeing if the renters in my home wanted to extend their stay, and working out all the details. But studying those photographs, I realized that I didn't want to live that far away from my family, from my daughters and granddaughter, maybe seeing them once a year. I loved my life in Aix, but I also could see the life that I had left back in California–my farm, my family, my friends–in a new light,

Royce and I had agreed that we'd suspend our relationship while I was in France; we were both free to date others. But we had a solid friendship based on open and honest communication and found ourselves having long conversations across the airwaves.

With the nine-hour time difference, I would call in the late afternoon and wake him up or he'd wake me up with a late night call before he went to bed. He knew how much this time in France meant to me and supported me in having the freedom to explore my life there without any ties.

As for me, I was enjoying the experience of just having male friends, *copains*, buddies, people I laughed and talked with, hung out with, but then left to stroll home to my place, alone.

Maybe it was my nineteen-year-old self, who had had to embrace marriage and motherhood before she was ready, who was running the show. But I didn't crave finding a partner during my time there. The person I most needed to find, get to know and love seemed to be myself.

There were some cute men around and we'd flirt a bit– European men are great flirts. But I wasn't moved to take it any further. I did meet a man at the church, who took me to lunch and commented on my *"accent charmant."* But even as we chatted over lunch, I was aware of the gaping cultural chasm between this devout Catholic Frenchman and me–with my wild Californian background and my only very recent reconnection to the Catholic Church.

His interest and attention were nice, but I knew we'd never get across that gap and I just wasn't motivated enough to try to bridge it. I'd smile and wave when I saw him, but sidestepped any more lunches.

So though my future article in a major New York magazine (my second New Millennium resolution) would carry the title, "My French Affaire," the life I was leading was not as racy as that suggested. And that suited me just fine.

While making my rounds of errands, I stopped in often at the church. Many days I would sneak in during the noon mass and sit in the back, soaking in the sound of the clear voices echoing off the arched ceiling, breathing in the fragrance of the incense, watching the light stream in from the green stained glass window and play on the walls. The scene evoked memories of my childhood, an innocent time when the mystery and timelessness of the rituals stirred a sense of wonder.

I appreciated this church, this haven and its connection to my past and to that of my ancestors, Catholics who had escaped Ireland during the potato famine in order to have the freedom to follow their faith. The monks emanated sincerity and goodness, faith in life, in mystery, in love, in the Divine and in destiny.

I let the gentle words of a sermon wash over me.

"*Ouvrez votre coeur, ressentir la paix, la partager avec les autres.*"

"Open your heart, feel the peace, share it with others."

One day, as I left the church, I picked up one of the weekly bulletins announcing all their activities and services. I noticed that one of the monks, was *un psychoanalyse*, a trained psycho-analyst. That got my attention because I found myself troubled and depressed after my mother's visit and also about the struggles with my former business partner. Later that day, I went around to the rectory to ask him if we could set up some times to talk. He agreed, and I began, once a week, to visit him in his office.

It was interesting to me that the problems I faced were the ones that I'd brought with me, from my past, from America. My life in Aix didn't present me with many difficulties larger than speaking French, dog poop and being careful crossing the street.

In my meetings with the monk, in the midst of the tears falling and the words tumbling out about my mother, my former business partner and my worries about money, a part of me stood back, triumphant and amazed, that I was able to have this level of conversation *in French*.

He listened and nodded, sympathetic and nurturing. He encouraged me to notice my strengths, how I'd come alone and had created a life there, speaking another language, and open to learning and growth. Most importantly, he told me that I needed to realize that I would never get from my mother what I longed to have, that she was incapable of giving it to me.

But I could let go now and move forward in my life, discovering my own inner source of love and nurturing. He also encouraged me to keep standing up to my former business partner to receive what I deserved. I could leave behind the sense of unworthiness that I had carried for so long. It was time to know my goodness, to stand in my light.

In other words, this monk became my own private angel. Week by week, I'd let his healing words, spoken in the soft and musical language that I so loved, seep in deep. After our time together, I'd leave lighter, sometimes even elated, as if I'd left the pain and sorrow wadded up in the tear soaked tissues, back in the trash can of his little office.

Of course I'd heard those words before and knew all that intellectually. But somehow, at that moment in my life, the words went in and stuck. Yes, I could let all of that go. And yes, I did feel stronger than when I arrived six months before. How wondrous, too, that this important piece of healing of long held traumas and demons was taking place with a monk, in France, in French.

My sister, safely home, wrote me a warm letter to thank me for her visit. She said she was in such a light and happy state when she left Aix and acknowledged me for where I was, being true to my heart; she said it gave me a charming vitality. I was so happy that I'd been able to share the magic of my life in Aix with Sharon and that it had mattered to her.

I never heard anything from my mother after her visit.

Tourists began to arrive, en masse, in Aix, always a stop on any self-respecting tour of Provence. They stood, maps in hand, cameras dangling, trying to find their way through the maze-like streets of the *vielle ville*. As I watched them arrive back at the central place, a bit bewildered that, *oh I'm here again*, I remembered how I'd also gotten lost on my first visit to Aix.

I had to laugh when I noticed how I resented their invasion of what, by now, seemed like my own private town in France. They clogged up the tiny streets, talking loudly to each other in English, or listening to a tour guide tell them about the history of the clock tower. I relished the fact that, at least for the moment, I was *not* a tourist, but *lived* in this beautiful corner of France.

However, living there, I'd discovered aspects of the hidden underbelly of Aix, one of which was a pair of female gypsies that stalked, tricked and robbed tourists. I'd seen them from time to time and had been warned about them, but now that *les Américains* had arrived, I saw them often.

They worked as a team, sneaking up on tourists. One of them would create a distraction, then the other one would pounce, deftly removing a wallet from a purse or backpack.

One day, as I sat at an outdoor café on *Cours Mirabeau*, I watched as they approached a couple of elderly women who were passing by on the sidewalk. The visitors were studying their map as the gypsies crept towards them. Just as the gypsies were about to strike the couple, I stood up. Moved by an energy that I didn't completely understand, I began to yell.

"Oh no you don't. I know what you're doing and you are *not* going to rob these women. Leave them. Go!"

From their confused expression, I realized that I was yelling at them, *in English*. I switched to French.

"*Non, non, arrettez-vous, maintenant. Laissez ces femmes. Allez!*"

And with that last word, I flung my arm out and glared at them. They were dumbfounded; first that I was yelling at them, which I'd already learned, no one did in public in France. And second, that I was willing to interrupt their little game to protect these women. I was taller than the gypsies, and definitely louder and they slunk away down the street. For once the tables were turned; they looked distracted and confused.

I explained to the tourists, who were clutching their cameras and purses, their maps dangling, what had just happened.

"Be careful. You are a target here for types like those. Watch out and if someone comes up to you, even groups of children, yell out '*NON*', and keep moving." They listened, nodded and then moved off, waving and thanking me.

As I sat back down at my place at the café, I noticed I was being stared at, but I didn't care. Maybe it was all the unfairness that I had endured from my mother, but I was unwilling to stand by and watch someone be violated like that. It had felt so good to deter those two thieves. And hey, I was an American. I was not ever going to be French, so they'd just have to get used to it.

My friend from the church was sitting at a nearby table. He

leaned over and, in a low voice, said that he thought what I'd done was admirable. "Those gypsies are a scourge in Aix," he said. "We are ashamed at what they do. You were right to stop them. It may not stop them for long, but at least you saved those two women."

I smiled, thanked him and as I finished my café, glanced down at my open journal. I'd copied down some words that morning from Willa Cather's book, *The Song of the Lark*.

> *I believe that the strongest need of your nature*
> *is to find yourself, to emerge as yourself.*

That was how it felt, like I was reclaiming lost parts and emerging as more of myself. How grand, that at age fifty-one, that could be happening. I closed up my book, smiled at the man from church and headed up the street to the market to do my shopping, the spring in my step reflecting new spaces of light and happiness.

Later that afternoon, I lined up with the other *Aixoise* at the Paul bakery, a few streets from my apartment. After the *bonjour* exchanged with the young woman behind the counter, I began my nightly speech, *"Une baguette a l'ancienne, bien cuite, s'il vous plaît."* An old recipe baguette, well done, please.

The bread, just lifted out of the wood-fired oven by a young man with a long wooden-handled spatula, felt warm and alive as I carried it home. The loaf, which had extra pointed edges, was crunchy on the outside, chewy on the inside. Many evenings, my dinner would consist of a glass of chilled white wine, a slice of tangy cheese, a tart apple and this bread. *Voila!* A delicious meal.

One evening, in addition to my usual baguette, I bought a lemon tart and a berry tart to share with Maïté, who was going to stop by for a late afternoon tea. She had to cancel and so, on a whim, I thought I'd just sample a bite of the lemon tart. It tasted so scrumptious that I took another and another and ended up eating it all. Then I looked at the berry one. Why not?

That was dinner that night. I felt full and satisfied and more than a little naughty, but very happy with my choices. As Garfield said, "Life is short, eat dessert first!"

During one of my many trips to the library at the American University in Aix, I met the director of the program. We then chatted several times during my visits. One day, she asked if I would like to give a talk to the students. I was doing my junior year abroad thirty years late—maybe I had some advice for them? Flattered, I agreed. Days later, I brought back some flyers to put up, announcing the talk.

"It's your Junior Year Abroad. Be sure to have the Time of Your Life," the flyers said. I thought that would get the students' attention.

The day of my talk, the bright-faced young students filled the room, with the director of the program sitting in the last row.

I told the group how I'd missed the chance to go when I was their age and had, at the age of fifty, set off to have the experience. I encouraged them to not just hang out with their American friends, speaking English, but to stretch and challenge themselves with the language, making French friends, going hours, days, as long as possible, in French.

I invited them to pay attention to what was different in France, the cultural differences, the manners, and of course the language. How was the experience of living as a student different in French, in France, from at home in America? I encouraged them to write in a journal, to note what they were feeling and experiencing. That some day, those words would be precious to them and, at that moment, writing could help them through some rough patches.

I said that homesickness was normal and to not be afraid of it. That right on the other side of it was a new, deeper sense of themselves, not just as an American student, or a sister or a brother, daughter or son, boyfriend or girlfriend—all of the ways they had identified themselves up to that point in their lives. I encouraged them to step out, that they were so much more than those identities, and that living abroad gave them a chance to get glimpses of those deeper parts and to grab hold of them.

I told them the story of how I found Gilbert, my father's orphan from World War II, and how that had solved part of the mystery of why I'd been so determined to learn French. I talked about how learning another language provided not only a good exercise for your brain; it broadened your horizons, and connected you to people you could never talk to otherwise.

I told them how this experience and time could change the course of their lives and how that was a good thing, not something to be afraid of. I recited Joseph Campbell's phrase, "Follow your bliss," and encouraged them to experience the bliss of this time away.

Above all, I told them, "Don't hold back. Have it all—and to be sure to have the time of your life."

Following my talk, they gathered around me, in wonder that a person so old could still be able to have a junior year abroad.

One young woman, told me how her boyfriend, afraid of losing her, kept calling and emailing. I encouraged her to gently try to free herself up more to be there, in France. She had the rest of her life to be in America, to be a girlfriend.

"Don't miss this chance, to learn more about who *you* are," I told her, "before you become an *us*." She nodded and listened.

The director shook my hand and thanked me, and as I headed back to my flat, I reminded myself that I too, was there to have the time of *my* life.

With the warmer weather, I needed to shed the hiking boots and long coat that had been my winter wardrobe. Luckily, I discovered a *Mephisto* store down a tiny alley, off *Cours Mirabeau*. The shop had comfortable sandals, even in my size, and I chose a blue suede pair, size *quarante-trois*, forty-three. I also found a short, lighter jacket, fitted and feminine, to replace by thick wool coat. A few cute t-shirts from *Etam* and *Voilà*! My new spring wardrobe.

19

She felt like a tree, bursting into bloom.
Willa Cather, *Song of the Lark*

Pâques: Easter

One of the features of my home in California, that I vowed never to take for granted again, was my washing machine. Or that I could dry my laundry outside, on a rope suspended between two trees.

In Aix, I was fortunate to have a *Laverie*, a Laundromat, right at the end of my block. Figuring out how to use the machines, however, proved more difficult. Luckily, there was a young person or two who helped me out the first few times till I knew the drill: Lots of coins, bring your own soap, and expect to wait a long time for the dryers, which must have been turned down very low, to make you keep feeding in the coins.

Ah well, I could buy a sandwich at the shop just a few doors down and eat it while I waited. This place made Paninis with the cheese and meat all melted together and *pommes frites* stuffed into the paper wrapping. I still felt wonder at all the treats I was able to enjoy because I ended up walking for two to three hours most days. In addition, the deliciousness of the food satisfied me and like the French, I didn't snack, so my clothes still fit with plenty of room.

Back at my apartment, I could hang a few items out to dry on my balcony, as my neighbors did. With the fresh, spring weather, I opened all the windows, letting the breeze ruffle my lace curtains, as my laundry dangled and swayed above the geraniums. Each week as I swept and mopped my apartment and did my laundry, I kept pinching my self at my good fortune. I tried not to think about the future, that I would have to leave this place. Right then, at that moment, it was perfect.

One spring day, as I swept and cleaned my apartment, I stepped out onto my tiny balcony, looked below and didn't see anyone, so shook out my dustbin of dirt and sand onto the street below. My young neighbor, the one who liked to blast his music so loud, was hidden below where I couldn't see him, smoking a cigarette. So, much to my *horreur*, the dirt went right onto his head.

A flurry of expletives came wafting up to me. I popped my head back out and called down, *"Oh! Excusez-moi, desolée, je ne pouvais pas vous voir."* Oh. Excuse me, I'm so sorry, I couldn't see you. But I couldn't suppress a giggle as I ducked back into my apartment. Maybe there *was* justice in the universe.

At Eastertime, it is a Provençal spring custom to grow fresh grass in a basket and Maïté showed me how: I bought a basket, lined it with paper towels, sprinkled in some seeds, and watered them each day. Sure enough, within a few weeks, I had a soft green lawn peeking up out of my basket, just inside my kitchen window.

In my hunt through the piles on the table at the open market, I found a hand embroidered tablecloth, decorated with Easter bunnies and eggs in soft, pastel colors. I put it onto my old pine table, placed my basket of grass in the center, threw in a few tiny colored eggs that I'd found at *Monoprix* and *Voilà!* I was ready for Easter and with it, my next guest, a friend named Dee.

Dee had been a part of the personal growth seminars I had organized for three years. Even though we didn't know each other that well, she felt like a sister. We were close in age, but Dee had waited to have children till she was almost forty, so had a seven-year-old son. She taught second grade and had never visited Europe. Her husband had agreed to look after their son so that she could fly across the Atlantic to spend her spring break with me, in France.

This was a wild and daring move for her and she arrived excited, exuberant and ready for fun. During her ten-day visit, we walked, lunched, caféd, shopped and giggled our way through Aix like a couple of schoolgirls.

I took her to the spa, which she adored. We ate lunch with Maïté at our favorite outdoor café, enjoying a huge chicken salad, bread, and a glass of wine for under ten dollars. We shopped for new clothes for her at *Etam*, complete with delicate and lacy under things, so that she could experience France from the inside out.

We drove to the Mediterranean with Maïté and hiked and swam. I took Dee to the church, to the open markets, and to the central place where we sipped a *grande crème* next to the fountain and under the plane trees. We sat at my old pine table and talked about all the changes I was going through. She marveled at my ability to speak French; when we were out, she'd pipe up and add '*bonjour*' and '*merci*.' I enjoyed experiencing Aix newly as she discovered it.

One nuance of French that made me chuckle was the local version of *"Ooh, là, là."* I'm not sure if this was the case only in the south of France, but it wasn't *"Ooh, là, là;"* what I heard was *"Err, là, là,"* accompanied by a frantic up and down motioning of the right hand, as if the speaker were strumming a banjo in front of her stomach.

I first noticed it with Maïté, then, as happens once you distinguish something new, began to see it all around me.

"Err, là, là," could express frustration about the traffic, such as *"Err, là, là, quelle circulation!"* Or it could be a dramatic expression about the rain. *"Err, là, là, je suis mouillée jusqu'aux os!"* I'm soaked to the skin! (Literally 'down to my bones'!) Or *"Err, là, là, quel crétin!"* Wow, what a jerk!

That was one of the fun *petits morceaux* of French that Dee learned when she visited. We did a lot of *Err, là, là-ing* together during those ten days, since everywhere we turned, Dee found so many things to exclaim about.

So in addition to *'bonjour,' 'merci'* and *'au revoir,'* she added *'Err, là, là,'* and *'magnifique'* to her French vocabulary. So much was magnificent that we had to also add that word.

At the end of her trip, I planned to take the train with her to Paris so that I could show her some of my favorite Parisian delights. We bought our tickets and packed a delectable lunch of wine, cheese, bread and fruit, with chocolate and raspberries for dessert.

In France, in spring, there's sometimes a phenomenon called *"la Grève,"* 'the strike.' The French are guaranteed the right to strike by their constitution, so even though it is a royal pain for visitors, they respect and validate their countrymen and women who are on strike and seem to be able to relax through the chaos which sometimes results.

The day Dee and I were to leave for Paris, the train conductors were on strike. Our local train from Aix left without a hitch but we arrived in Marseilles to a scene of pure pandemonium. It wasn't clear which train was going where or at what time.

I checked the overhead sign, which told us platform C3 for our train to Paris. Minutes later, the sign went blank, with no new information.

Dee and I got on the train at C3, found our seats and stowed the lunch and our bags. She began to make friends with the man in the seat across the aisle, as she always did in her friendly way, and he was happy to practice his English. I said that I was just going to run and check to make sure that this was the right train—I'd be right back. No one knew when the train was going to leave because no conductors were in sight and the overhead sign was empty. Her new friend told us that he'd been waiting for hours.

I jumped off and ran through the crowds to the office, trying to get the attention of someone to ask about our train. The line moved slowly but when I was able to ask my question, I discovered that no, that train was not our train to Paris. We should have been on the train at D4. The harried young woman wasn't sure where the train at C3 was going.

I wove my way back through the throngs of bewildered travelers as fast as I could, to tell Dee that we had to gather up our things and move to the other train. I pushed through the crowd and arrived at C3 and I froze. C3 was empty: no train. Open space and empty tracks stretched out ahead, disappearing in the distance.

In a very loud voice, I said "Oh, my God," and put my hand up to my mouth. People standing nearby turned to look, and stared with raised eyebrows. I had again broken two rules, to yell out loud and to do so in English.

The train was gone, and Dee with it, along with my bags, my ticket, and the lunch. I had my small purse/backpack with about 50ff in it—about $7. But the scariest part was that I didn't know *where* that train was going. I ran back to the woman at the counter. She thought maybe Brussels.

Dee, who at that moment was speeding through the French countryside without me, had no way to reach me. She didn't even have the name of the hotel where we were staying in Paris. She also spoke hardly a word of French. If she *was* headed to Brussels, how would I ever find her again? I shivered at that thought.

I walked back to C3 and stood and stared. Maybe if I looked long enough, the train would somehow materialize in front of me and it would all be a dream. Maybe if I waited, the train would reappear around the corner, backing up into the station, coming back for me.

But it was gone. No amount of staring was going to bring it back. I stumbled over to the train to Paris at D4 and boarded. With no ticket, I picked a random seat; I didn't know which seat I was supposed to have. As the train moved out of the station, I stared out the window, trying to imagine Dee's reaction. She must have been in some kind of shock and disbelief as the train left without me. At least she had her new friend to talk to and he spoke English.

I had to take some action. Above all, I had to try to find out where Dee's train was going. So I asked the server in the restaurant car whether there were any conductors or officials on board. He said there was one up in First Class. I thanked him and wove my way through the cars till I found the conductor, alone in the First Class car.

He was on strike, hiding out. He didn't want to talk to me, I was sure. But I had to try.

"Excusez-moi, monsieur. Mais j'ai un grand problème." Excuse me sir, but I have a *big* problem. He looked up, raised an eyebrow, then motioned for me to sit.

I fell into the seat facing him and proceeded to pour out my story, in the best French I could muster. How Dee was on the other train, speeding somewhere. The bags, the tickets and most of all, the *lunch* were speeding along with her. (I knew that fact should inspire his sympathy.) And the *'pièce de résis-tance'*–exactly *where* was she speeding *to*?

He listened to all of it, then smiled a little, looking me up and down, as if he were sizing me up. He could tell I hadn't made up the story. It was too wild and silly to be made up.

Alors. Alright then. That great French word when you are gathering your thoughts.

He stood up and made a motion for me to follow him. By some kind of luck, the petite Frenchman in his gray conductor's uniform, who was on strike, became my partner. For the next hour and a half, I followed him like a shadow, up and down train aisles, from car to car. We ventured into the hidden niches and crannies of a speeding TGV train–closets and cubbyholes with phones, schedules and timetables.

He leafed through thick books with tiny print and numbers, mumbling to himself, then would look up and ask me a question.

Did I know the number of the train she was on? *"Non."* The number of the track it had left from? *"Oui. C3."* The time it left–approximately. From time to time I'd sigh and moan–what if she was on her way to Brussels!

After many phone calls and much muttering over train schedules, he discerned that her train was, after all, going to Paris and would arrive about the same time as ours. (Though we had departed a bit later, our high-speed train traveled faster than her train.) What relief! I thanked him profusely, before we parted ways. He smiled, shook my hand and invited me to sit in First Class.

I spent my 50ff on a Heineken and a packet of cookies, all I could buy with my meager monies and settled into a comfortable seat in the empty First Class car.

Sipping my beer and looking out the window as France sped by, I started to laugh. Just when you think you have it all worked out, life throws you a curve ball, to remind you that you are not in charge, really.

But the fact was, Dee was fine, I was fine, and we were both on our way to Paris, just on different trains! And she had the lunch. Knowing Dee, she was enjoying the fine bread and cheese, wine, chocolate and raspberries with her new friend. I crunched my cookies.

The train announced its presence with a 'whoo whoo.' I sat back in the seat and tried to relax. The ever-changing scenery outside the train window was, as always, fascinating. Farmlands and villages, then someone's back yard garden with neat rows of cabbages, lettuces and white sheets fluttering in the spring breeze. Sunlight slanted off church steeples and the cars on the roads seemed to be in slow motion compared to our high-speed train.

I arrived in Paris a few minutes ahead of Dee's train and ran to meet it, weaving through the crowd, searching for her. Then I saw her coming towards me, her new friend helping her with my bag. When she saw me, she let out a whoop. We ran toward each other, squealed, hugged and jumped up and down. At that moment, I didn't care that we were making a scene, breaking all the rules of correct French conduct. We cried, we laughed, we talked fast.

"I didn't know what to do," she said. "I couldn't believe it when the train started to move and you weren't there. I kept saying, 'Oh my god, oh my god'."

"I know, I know. I was so panicked when I came back and looked down those empty tracks," I said. "Then I thought you might be going to Brussels! And you had the lunch!"

"I know. It was so good," she said. "I saved you some chocolate."

We sat and shared a glass of wine with her new friend until we calmed down a little. He had planned to take her home if

I didn't show up in Paris. I'm not sure how I would have ever found her then. But never mind. Somehow, it all had turned out so well. We sipped our wine, euphoric that, after such a major detour, our trip to Paris was 'back on track.'

Outside the train station, we grabbed a cab, a Mercedes. The taxi driver smiled as he seated us in the plush back seat. Dee and I were both still so grateful and excited that we had found each other that we were giddy.

He drove us through the Paris streets and across the Seine toward our hotel in the Latin Quarter as the Beatles song, "Can't Buy Me Love" blasted from the radio. We rolled down the windows and sang along as the lights of Paris sped by and the warm spring air carried our voices and the music out into the night.

At the hotel, the driver helped us with our bags, and we waved goodbye to him; I think our exuberance made his day. In spite of all that could have gone wrong, by some grace, we were safe at our hotel, together, in Paris. We walked arm in arm down *Boulevard St. Michel*, visited *Notre Dame*, strolled along the Seine and then enjoyed steak and *pommes frites* with a *demi pichet* of red wine at a sidewalk bistro.

The next morning, Dee took a cab to the airport and flew back to her normal life, back to teaching second grade, back to her husband and son, full of the wonder of the time that we'd shared.

I took the train back to Aix, cherishing my life in France and the two months that I had left to enjoy it.

20

*The things that were really hers
separated themselves from the rest.
She felt united and strong.*
Willa Cather, *Song of the Lark*

Mai: May

Each Sunday during the winter and spring, I'd gone hiking with my friends. We'd driven to the Var, a region near Aix, and hiked to the cave where many believed Mary Magdalene spent the last days of her life. Murals on the chapel walls depicted vivid images of her landing in France and of her time there. The chapel, like so many holy places in France, felt cool, quiet and sacred.

Many weeks, we hiked along the Calanques, long, narrow fjords that wove along the shore near the village of Cassis, a half hour from Aix. As the weather warmed, we'd swim in the water after our hikes and picnics. By May, we were going to the beach often, a group of us piling into cars and meeting at the shore to swim, picnic and relax.

I felt like a teenager. I didn't have a car, caught rides, and hung out at the beach, carefree and relaxed. After six months of living in France, I was also aware of how much the French were not Puritans, which so contrasted with my own rigid American heritage.

For one thing, it was perfectly acceptable for me to take my top off at the beach. Back in California, I'd have been arrested *immédiatement* for indecent exposure, but in France, no one even noticed. One day, after swimming and lunch, we'd changed and left our bathing suits in the car. The group then decided to take a long walk down the beach and I found myself longing to go into the water again. So I asked Maïté if it would be all right if I took another dip in my undies, since I didn't have my bathing suit.

Mais Oui! Of course, she said, looking surprised that I even had to ask. So I took off my shorts and top, jumped into the water and enjoyed another delightful swim. Back up onto the beach, I sat and dried off in the sun, then put my clothes on again and that was that. *Pas de problème!* No problem. No one even glanced my way.

Once a week, a retired professor of French held a small, intimate conversation class in her home just outside of Aix. I could catch a bus on the *Cours Mirabeau* and after a fifteen-minute ride out into the country, get dropped off right near her home.

So each week, I'd catch the bus and walk to her home to sit with four or five others in her formal living room and fall under the scrutiny of her very particular French oral sensibility. Although she was in her seventies, and officially retired after teaching for decades, she seemed to enjoy her classes. She was rather stern in her corrections, both of pronunciation and of grammar, so I thought carefully before I opened my mouth.

But even when I did, I was sure to be corrected, usually with regards to my accent. *Madame, le professeur,* did not consider my American accent to be *charmant* but, rather, an annoyance that had to be set right; she was determined to correct it out of me.

But that was fine. I needed lots of correction. I could even hear my own accent. There was just such a long way to go in mastering a second language.

Even with the sometimes discouraging aspects of her classes, it was a privilege to sit with this elegant and distinguished matron and guardian of the French language and pass muster at all. Beneath her somewhat severe exterior, she was kind and even a bit friendly at times.

One evening, at the end of class, she smiled at me. *"Vous vous débrouillez très bien et vous faites des progrès. Continuer!"* You are doing very well, and making progress. Continue on! Those words made me so happy that I almost skipped back to the bus stop.

I *was* doing very well, finding my way inside of my beloved language, which, even after so many years of study and practice, remained a continuing challenge. I *liked* the challenge. At the half-century point of my life, how wondrous to be learning something new every single day. Living inside of the French language required an alertness that, while sometimes tiring, was also rewarding. By now, I had also become accustomed to the level of vulnerability that it demanded.

And I *liked* her, the French version of myself, who walked the cobblestone streets carrying her woven basket full of vibrant fresh produce, a baguette poking out of one end, and a colorful bouquet of flowers at the other. I felt excited by life, by the newness that presented itself to me around every corner. Even in my daily routines, there were so many surprises.

Yes, *je me suis débrouillée,* I was managing, coping, making my way.

Living in France *inside* of the French language, gave me a glimpse into the culture that I could never have experienced any other way. I could feel the sensibilities of the culture, the subtle manners, some of which we had lost in America. In the supermarket, you'd say, '*Oh, pardon,*' if you came even close to someone else's personal space.

There were, of course, the rules about not yelling in public or making a scene, rules I'd broken at different times during my stay. I enjoyed the simple ritual of greeting and being greeted by the shop owner when I entered a shop, and then saying goodbye and thank you when I left. All was done in an unhurried and polite manner.

Those may seem like small things, but as the months went by, I could feel my own reactions, along with the locals, when tourists, mostly Americans, broke those subtle cultural conventions. I could see why we'd become labeled as 'Ugly Americans' for being too loud, too pushy, and, in their terms, too impolite. I was grateful I'd been able to merge into the culture as well as I had and never took that for granted.

I had made friends with another '*madame le professeur,*' a woman my age, an elementary grade teacher. One day, she invited me to come to her class to speak to the children, to help them to practice English. In the formal classroom atmosphere, the uniformed students sat quietly, raised their hands to speak, then stood and addressed the teacher in a polite way.

This '*madame le professeur*' was also stern and I began to sense that this may be the way teaching was done in France. My high school French teacher, Mr. Maiwald, was German, but spoke impeccable French. He ruled the classroom with an iron hand, but I thrived in his class. He made it clear what you had to do to succeed: learn it all, every nuance of every irregular verb ending, accent or vocabulary word. Luckily, I *wanted* to learn it all, so he and I got along just fine.

When Gilbert DesClos and his family came to visit us

in California a few years before, I took them to my nephew Brendan's sixth grade class. Romain, Gilbert's twelve-year-old grandson, sat in on the class, even though he didn't speak English, then joined the soccer game at lunchtime. At the end of the school visit, Romain announced that he was coming to live in California—the kids had way more fun at school than they did in France.

Looking at my friend's class and comparing that to the more relaxed atmosphere of my nephew's class, I had to agree with Romain. I wasn't sure which approach got the best results. Maybe the California system worked for our more open-minded lifestyle. But the contrast gave me something to think about as I headed back to my apartment after my visit to the classroom that day.

Through all of this, I'd been continuing my once-a week sessions with the monk. His gentle and kind words helped me to sort through the issues that had followed me all my life, like dark shadows.

For many years I'd felt angry at how I'd arrived at adulthood completely unequipped for the challenges facing me. My parents had been terrible models for how to have a healthy relationship and I had struggled with both self-confidence and self-esteem. I had always excelled in school, never needing a remedial course. But for a long time, I wished there were a remedial course in how to do *life*.

With the perspective of my time in France, many things were becoming clear. For one, in a perfect world, everyone would be happy and confident. But it wasn't a perfect world. Everyone, it seemed, had something to heal. I wasn't the only one.

The monk and I talked about my recent business partnership, in which my confidence, my sense of dignity and self-worth had all been damaged. I'd felt used up and then discarded, exploited and then thrown away.

Le frère helped me to be with the anger and emotions, so they could pass through me and lead to a place of healing and opening. The distance and time away from home allowed me to have the perspective to see both the strong points of my life, and the weak points. I needed to let go of a lot and I needed to learn to choose better.

Like in a poker hand, I could keep the aces and discard the two of clubs. My sister, daughters, grandbaby, some special friends, my organic farm, France, French, and writing were all keepers. I felt ready to let go of other pieces my life, like critical and unsupportive people. Also, working for others; I needed to focus on my own work, writing and coaching.

Le frère helped me learn to look for my strengths, to listen, and to pray. And suddenly, in the midst of this deep healing, across the planet, my former business partner shifted and paid me what he owed me. I took that as a sign that in this inner journey, I'd made some progress.

The French have a saying, *"Je suis bein dans ma peau."* I feel good in my skin. I could feel that now. Like a butterfly, I'd had real struggles to get out of the cocoon that had been both comfortable and stifling. I felt ready to fly.

Once or twice a week, a group of us attended a movie. Sometimes we saw an American movie, such as *Erin Brockovitch* or *American Beauty*, but usually it was a French film, with no subtitles, of course. As good as my French had become, I still struggled with television and movies–it all moved so fast and the characters often used slang that I didn't know.

In the same way, Maïté had trouble with American movies. In *Erin Brockovitch*, where the character used a lot of slang, Maïté missed a lot, (though they had French subtitles). But for me, to watch an American movie in English was like a miracle, a short rest for my brain from living in French.

Many European movies showed immigrants on ships going to America. The passengers would crowd onto the decks searching for signs of land. When they spotted the Statue of Liberty, they'd cry and scream in joy, "America!" Their voices held such longing and wonder and I could feel again what America represented to the world: a place to have a fresh start, the new world. I wiped away some tears during those moments, grateful for the dark theater.

By this time, I could see how I would always be American; I would never be French. Even if I could master the language, I would have an accent that would give me away. I would continue to be a bit too big for the country, for their beds, their shoes and almost, their clothes.

But I felt a new peace with myself. I was not a delicate little flower. I was more like a strong horse, thanks to my good old American gene pool, which included some very tall Danes.

I had American friends who, in spite of living in France for many years, spoke French so badly that it grated on my own ears, and I could only imagine what it did to French ones. It sounded as if they were speaking English, but saying French words–they hadn't adopted the French intonation.

Other Americans spoke English with a French accent, which seemed incredibly affected. They had morphed into a persona that was neither French nor American and their speech seemed to reflect their own confusion about who they were.

French was not my first language. To pretend that it was, would be like playing a part in a play. And since I wanted to live an authentic life, it felt good to know who I was, an American, who spoke polite French. I didn't know much slang, if any, so probably came across as rather formal, even old fashioned. But that worked well in the culture.

Even without much slang, my fluency made French seem like one of two channels in my brain. Sometimes I would not know if I was speaking French or English and I could switch back and forth; I was even dreaming in French. English was the stronger frequency, for sure, but the other channel, French, was rich, exotic and true, taking its place in my life, claiming its place in my heart and mind.

I no longer wanted to be French. I just wanted to be me.

21

Fortune may not soon pass this way again
and this moment in time—never again.

Phil Cousineau, *The Art of Pilgrimage*

La Visite d'Ellie: "Doucement"
Ellie's Visit: "Gently, easily, tenderly, carefully, slowly"

My daughter Michelle and her husband Claude were bringing my granddaughter Ellie over for a visit at the end of May, so I began to clean and prepare my apartment for a nine-month old. I swept and mopped, getting underneath the couch and bed, trying to see the world from the vantage point of a crawling baby.

There was no way I could 'baby-proof' my apartment. The old building had wires sticking out of plugs and ancient water pipes; I'd need to buy bottled water for sure. But I borrowed a high chair, bed and stroller and stocked up on some French baby food and disposable diapers.

However, in the world of French baby food, unlike the American version, there was no such thing as just 'carrots' or 'squash.' The French spiced up the vegetable with onions and herbs. To their gourmet sensibilities, it must have been a crime to serve plain carrots, even to a baby. I wasn't sure how little Ellie's stomach would adjust to such culinary innovations, but I bought it because that was all that they had.

In the diaper department, her size put her into toddler pull-up diapers. Just like her *grandmère*, she was a giant in the country, even at nine months.

I waited for them at the gate at the Marseilles airport and when Ellie saw me, she smiled. She hadn't seen me for over seven months–an eternity in her short life. I was so happy and held them all close. We stuffed their luggage, Ellie in the car seat, and the three of us into Maïté's car; I'm not sure how we fit it all in, but we did.

After settling them in a nearby hotel, we went walking with Ellie in the stroller. She was all mixed up with the time change and slept most of the day, even as her stroller bumped along the cobblestones. In the open market, we bought olives and bread, fruit and nuts. We ate lunch at my favorite restaurant, then walked to the church. I showed them my apartment and we had tea. By then Ellie was awake and sat in the high chair.

Later, as we pushed Ellie again through the winding streets, I had to laugh. For the young students doing their junior year abroad, their parents came to visit them. In my case, my daughter, son-in-law and granddaughter had come to visit me.

I thought about my father's time in France before I was born and how I grew up hearing his stories. Now, Ellie represented the fourth generation in my family to experience the chatter of French, the tolling of the church bells, and the cobblestone streets of France.

Michelle and Claude spent three days in Aix, giving Ellie a chance to get comfortable with me and the apartment. Then my daughter and her husband took off to Italy for ten days for a second honeymoon. I'd offered to take Ellie so they could have that time together, and now it was just my granddaughter and me.

It became clear right away that when Ellie was awake we had to get out of the apartment. My plants, at just the right height, became irresistible targets for her to pull out the dirt and try to eat it. The wires sticking out of the plugs drew her like a magnet. So as soon as she woke up, after a snack and a diaper change, we'd head down the stairs and out into Aix.

People on the street would stop and exclaim, *"Oh, elle est tellement belle!"* Oh, she is so beautiful. Ellie didn't know the difference between French and English, but responded to their smiles and warmth. We discovered playgrounds, marveled at the fountains, and drove to the Mediterranean with a friend and her young daughter.

When we'd return from shopping, I'd run her up the three flights of stairs and strap her into her into her high chair where she would be safe, then bound down and come back up with the groceries, then again with the bottled water. She'd laugh as I burst through the door, thinking it was all just a game of peek-a-boo.

Carrying a twenty-two pound baby up and down those stairs provided a lot of exercise. But the main thing I noticed was how much being with her opened my heart. Her pure innocence and trust inspired me to handle all the challenges of being in charge of her for ten days. She didn't cry or whine for her parents, but seemed to accept that I was there to take care of her.

I gave up on trying to get her to sleep in the baby bed and just put her into my bed next to me. I'd fall into bed when she did, tired from all the exertion of caring for her. The quality of sleep wasn't the greatest, but I gained in other ways. During the night, if she woke up and started fussing, she'd reach over and feel my face with her tiny hands. I'd reach back and pat her, and she'd relax again, sprawling her tiny body and chubby feet and arms all over, her breathing becoming quiet and steady as she fell back to sleep.

The selflessness and devotion required in caring for her, was like a meditation. Her smiles and laughter were gifts and a reminder of what a miracle of life she was. How lucky we were to now have her in our family.

Gilbert and Huguette came to visit while Michelle and Claude were away and stayed with me in the apartment. They admired my home and enjoyed exploring Aix and we all cooked together in my kitchen. Ellie smiled and laughed in the midst of life happening in French.

One of my very favorite words in French is *doucement*. It means 'gently, easily, tenderly, carefully, slowly.'

The first time the word *doucement* registered in my brain had been six years before, when Heather and I were visiting Paris. We were at Montmartre and Heather, nineteen, wanted to jog up to the top of the grand staircase and back down. She did so, springing along effortlessly, her strong long legs carrying her up, up, up.

I, on the other hand, huffed and puffed. Many of the people on the stairs looked at us with wide eyes, these two exuberant and maybe a bit crazy Americans as we jogged and giggled up and down the stairs.

These stairs have one of the most powerful views of Paris—all the way across the city to the Eiffel Tower in the distance, with the Seine snaking along, dividing Paris into the 'right bank' and the 'left bank.' The early evening cool breeze hit my sweaty body as I stopped to take in the view. A group of young men, lounging along the rail near the bottom, decided to engage us, or at least try to engage Heather, in conversation.

"Eh Voilà! La jeune fille va très vite et la mamma, elle vient plus doucement." Hey look, the daughter goes fast and her mama, well, she comes along more *doucement*.

At that moment, I heard *doucement*. Not *lentement*, which I had learned for slowly, but *doucement*. I thought they meant slowly, yet it was obviously different. When I looked it up in my dictionary later that night in our hotel, I discovered the distinction: It meant 'gently, easily, tenderly, carefully, and finally, slowly.'

After that, every time someone said *doucement*, I heard it and understood. You touched a baby *doucement*. You handled something fragile, *doucement*. If you twisted your ankle and had to gingerly stand on it, it would be *doucement*. If you inquired about someone who died, you'd say you hoped it had all happened *doucement*.

When I took care of Ellie, I heard the word *doucement* all the time. To my young friend Natalie's three-year-old as she touched Ellie, her mother pleaded *"doucement, si tu plaîs."* I'd lift a sleeping Ellie or lay her down, *doucement*. As Ellie bounced up and down in her borrowed playpen and threatened to push the floor out of it, Huguette laughed to her, *"Ellie, plus doucement, si tu plaîs."*

I felt a thrill of pleasure each time I heard that word and understood the subtle distinction it communicated. What a different world, from just 'slowly.'

Maïté corrected me *doucement* when I used a wrong word, substituting the correct word; I did the same for her in English. It felt satisfying to help each other like that, gently teaching each other the nuances of our respective languages. My more formal French friends would never consider correcting me, nor I them. But Maïté and I had a sisterly understanding and ease that allowed us to help each other, *doucement*.

When Michelle and Claude came back and Ellie and I opened the door, Ellie seemed stunned for a moment, then smiled and wiggled in delight. *Oh yeah, grandma and I were fine, but here's Mommy and Daddy again. Oh yes!* After their joyful reunion, the next time I held her, she hung onto me with her little fists tight on my arms and pushed her body up to me–a baby hug. I was so happy.

We went down to Cassis to stay the night, where we watched the fishing boats return in the morning with their catch, then swam in the Mediterranean in the afternoon. We had a new level of closeness, intimacy and play between all of us. Everyone let down their guard with Ellie around.

Then it was time to say goodbye again. It was now early June and I had less than a month left of my stay in France.

22

Artistic growth is, more than it is anything else,
a refining of the sense of truthfulness.

Willa Cather, *The Song of the Lark*

Juin: June

After my family and Gilbert and Huguette left, the apartment felt so quiet. I slept in, catching up on the days of exertion and nights of lost sleep with Ellie. I relished my freedom again, to write and to go out whenever I wanted, but I also missed my family. Taking care of my granddaughter and feeling the connection with her made me certain that I didn't want to live so far across the planet, seeing her maybe once a year.

During those days alone again, as I looked back at my time in France, I felt a tremendous sense of peace.

I had missed out on this experience of living abroad in my youth, but now that I had experienced it, there was no longer a gap. I had come in search of my nineteen-year-old self and now realized that I had never lost her.

The turn my life had taken at nineteen, which had sometimes felt out of control was, as I looked back, exactly what needed to have happened in order to be who I was, in that moment. The question of who I might have been if I had come to France at nineteen was laid to rest. I felt whole and happy to be me, just as I was, a fifty-one year old American, with two daughters, a granddaughter and, if I was lucky, close to another half century of life still ahead of me.

Instead of looking at myself as a more diminished version of who I could have been, I felt proud of who I was. How rich my life had been and how full. I was ready to go back and start again with a renewed sense of hope. And with a sense of peace about the choices I had made all those years ago.

Maybe my life wouldn't ever make the pages of *Who's Who in American Women*. Or I wouldn't be on the cover of some magazine or invited to the White House. But I had an amazing life.

For all of the heartaches and pain, failures and successes, it had turned out. The imaginary 'other life' couldn't begin to compare to what I had actually lived during those thirty years of waiting; not some picture perfect illusion, but a *real* life.

At fifty, I came to France to discover and to discern who I was deep down, underneath my family, my history, my culture and language, my past and my programming. The essential self, who had a purpose and a destiny—I went to France to find her. And I did. That is not a journey I could have taken at nineteen.

And the wonder is that I discovered that my dream of living in France had become richer from cherishing it for so long. It had become richer in the waiting.

My second 'new millennium resolution' of getting published in a major New York magazine came through during those last few weeks. I'd sent a pitch to *More* magazine, a new magazine for women 'of a certain age' (over forty), and they had accepted my story, "My French Affaire, My Junior Year Abroad Thirty Years Late."

My monk and I completed our sessions with some tears

on my part. The time with him had not only been healing personally, it had also allowed me to reconnect with the church of my childhood.

In my last session, I asked him about the church's position on remarriage. I hoped to find my partner and possibly get married again and it made me sad that the church would condemn that. He answered that yes, though the church held that position, he would be happy to bless us if we came to him. I felt comforted and grateful.

I had one more visitor before I left. My best friend Janna, who'd been so supportive during the difficult first few months. We'd talked often on the phone and she'd always reminded me to believe in myself, to *'croyez-en-soi.'*

She arrived with her family at the end of June and we shared the pleasures of my life in Aix and the wonder and joy of how well it had all turned out. Her daughter took some photos of me in front of the old clock tower in the main plaza, One of them ended up illustrating the article in *More* magazine.

My passport was due to expire one day before I left France, so I applied to renew it at the closest American Consulate, in Marseilles. The renewal form had a space for 'permanent address.' As I filled it out, grateful to have my farm as a 'permanent address,' I realized I was ready to go home, to begin my life again, in America.

My new passport arrived, issued by *le Conseil Général de Marseilles*, the American Consulate in Marseilles. My American passport was 'half French,' a small souvenir of my time in France.

Taking apart my apartment was daunting. I shared the geraniums among my friends. I packed up boxes with the curtains, sheets, pillows and towels to give to Maïté. If I returned, I could borrow them back. Maïté gave me a giant suitcase, and

I packed the antique linens, plates and wine glasses in with my clothes. A group of friends threw me a farewell party and we all promised to stay in touch. We went to the beach as many times as possible in those last few weeks, savoring the cool water as the temperatures began to soar.

Now that it was June, Aix became even more crowded with tourists. I was so happy that I had lived there during the off season, when I had been one of the locals going about life in the narrow, cobblestone streets.

Trusting and believing in myself had been the right mantras for the journey that I had been on. Those new strengths were priceless gifts that I could take home with me to California.

In many of my visits to France, I had attended special sound and light shows during the summer season. They were called *"Son et Lumière,"* 'sound and light' and were held at places of historical significance, such as Mont St. Michel and castles in the Loire valley. The old buildings emanated an aura of mystery and magic, as light reflected off the ancient walls and soft music played in the background.

I had a private name for my time in France, *"le son et lumière de mon âme,"* the sound and light of my soul. I had settled into myself more deeply and had a clearer sense of who I was, of the sound and light of my soul.

I could stand back and honor the strength I'd had, to arrive in Aix, knowing no one and to find my way, make friends and find my home. I'd achieved my goal of fluency in French, from my eight months of immersion and loved the language even more. My writing career had taken a leap and I'd achieved my new years resolutions.

I felt younger and freer than when I'd arrived, softer and yet stronger at the same time.

If I could fulfill this long held desire, what else could I do?

I was returning to my old life, but not as the same person who had left.

I'd learned to read the international news and had gained a wider, global perspective. More than ever, I could see that we all share one small, fragile planet and all of its resources. The European way of life, with their tiny cars, fast trains and public transportation, was doing a much better job at conserving those resources; America lagged way behind in that scenario. I could see that we needed to learn to 'play well with others' as the Europeans had, as they co-existed in the European Union.

Fifty years of conditioning in one language, English, one culture, America, with all our idiosyncrasies, created a personality and expectations that definitely got jarred when uprooted to another alien soil. But I had *wanted* to experience that. I had *wanted* to try to get down under who I was as an American and discover who I was, in French. It was only one step further, to go down to who I was, period.

Living in France, struggling in my second language, learning to adapt to the cultural differences, I'd had to be vulnerable. I was returning home with a new respect for and honoring of vulnerability.

I was also returning to America with a new appreciation of what it meant to be an American. That appreciation came from seeing America from afar, what parts of American culture I cherished and which parts of the old world I wanted to reclaim.

I was from both the old world and the new world. All Americans were from somewhere 'old world' originally, except for the Native Americans. I now went out into the world as citizen of the world, then American. Like Family, tree, Genus, oak.

I felt embarrassed by Mc Donalds, our violent movies and the way that our consumerism machine gobbled up smaller cultures, which France and other European countries feared.

But I could now see how we had an open mindedness, a

tolerance for differences and a value of hard work, all of which I appreciated. True, we'd taken the value of hard work too far and become workaholics, losing *l'art de vivre,* the 'art of living' that the French did so well. But in America, a person could make something of him or herself from drive and desire. In America, a person could reinvent him or herself.

We valued independence, free thinking and thinking outside of the box. And the sheer size of our physical space encouraged and reinforced us to do that.

Most French were astounded that I came alone, for eight months, to a town I'd only visited once for two days, where I knew no one. That was an American kind of risk to take, with no formal introductions to open doors. My 'American-ness' had allowed me to pull it off.

I could see all of that now and had both pride and shame about who we were in the world. That left me wondering, how could we take the good parts of what we have and improve where we needed to?

In an ideal world, everyone would live in another country, long enough to get homesick and long enough to see his or her own country from afar.

23

*Sometimes, it turns out, you have to travel a long
distance to find your way back home.*
Pilar Guzmán, Editor in chief, *Condé Nast Traveler*

Le Retour: The Return

I left the apartment sparkling, wanting to remember it the
way it had been on that very first day, when I had made
it my own. Then I turned the big, rusty key in the lock and
headed down the three flights of stairs for the last time.

Maïté drove me to the Marseille airport and we said a
tearful goodbye, promising to keep in touch and to visit. In
Paris, I boarded the big jet for the long flight home. Settling
back into my seat on United Airlines, listening to the flight
attendant's announcements, I realized that I was now reenter-
ing 'life in English.'

When I landed in San Francisco, Royce met me to drive me
back to the farm. The next morning, as we entered a bakery,
the first thing I noticed in my jet-lagged haze, was that no one
greeted us. No, *"bonjour madame."* Oh, right, I thought. This
is America.

At that moment, I also realized that my newly attained

fluency in French, which I had worked so hard to achieve, was about to go dormant, to no longer be a part of my day-to-day life. *Merde!* Damn! (One bit of slang that I did know.)

I moved back into my house, but it took weeks to begin to find my way again. I was experiencing culture shock in the other direction now, feeling the loss of my life in France while trying to reestablish my life in California.

I ran into friends who expressed surprise that I was back already. *Already?* It seemed to me like I'd been gone an eternity. Their life didn't seem to have changed a bit, yet I felt so different. Could I fit back into my old life? And did I even *want* to do that?

I wrote a lot, trying to sort out what I could do with this new life and self I'd uncovered in France. I visited my daughters and granddaughter often, loving that we were all in the same country, state and time zone. I wrote for the local paper, cared for my farm, and experienced my quiet life in the country from a new perspective.

My farm felt like an old friend, welcoming me back, as if saying, *bring it all back here, to this land. You will sort it out.* And I did, day-by-day, week-by-week, and month-by-month.

I found that the person I'd become in my journey to France helped me to live a richer life than the one I'd left behind. Bringing my new self back into my old surroundings let me see how different I was, more calm and peaceful. Those qualities helped me through the re-entry transition.

Maïté and I stayed in touch, and, the following summer, she came to visit. She marveled at my different personality, in English; she had only known me in French, in France, far from home. In California, surrounded by friends and family, without the uncertainty of speaking a second language, I was more self-assured and confident. I helped her with English as we visited garage sales, which she loved, swam in mountain lakes and rivers, and explored my little mountain town.

The next summer, I returned to Aix for a few days to write and to visit old friends. When I stopped into the AAGP meeting on a Thursday morning, it was as though I had never left.

I slipped back into my French life, for those few days. The man selling roasted chicken and potatoes at the open market remembered me and, as before, gave me the extra crispy potatoes.

The seller with the embroidered tablecloths shook my hand, and I lined up again for my *baguette à l'ancienne, bien cuit* at the Paul bakery on *Rue Espariat.* I returned to the church and even had a meeting with my special monk.

I walked to *Rue des Bernadines* and looked up at my apartment, but it was dark and shuttered. It looked so lonely, with no geraniums on the balcony, no lace curtains fluttering at the window.

As I stood and stared up at what had been my home, I wondered, had it all been a dream? But I knew the answer in every fiber of my being: No, it had been real. It had been one of the most real experiences of my life and at the half century point, that was saying something.

In Aix, I had grown and changed, healed and matured, laughed and cried. I blessed my sweet home and wished it well, and as I walked away, I experienced again the place that opened up in me, that I could only access in France, in French.

The mystery of that enthralled me. It is what I felt all those years ago, sitting on my bed and listening to my sister's friend utter *chambre meublée.* I had sensed a world that wanted to pull me into it, a rich and safe place where some other, undiscovered part of me could emerge.

My eight-month sojourn gave me that missing piece of the puzzle that I'd been waiting to find for thirty years.

I give thanks now, for the road not taken at twenty and for the road taken thirty years later. I discovered that there is no "late." There is only "now."

And that my Junior Year Abroad was not thirty years late. It was right on time.

L'Épilogue: Epilogue

Over sixteen years have passed since I embarked on my eight-month adventure of living in France. I still hold that time as one of the most powerful and enriching experiences of my life and feel deep gratitude that I was able to have it.

I was left with the question that if I could fulfill that long cherished wish, what other dreams could I dust off and have? What other important experiences could lay just beyond my comfort zone?

That inquiry has led me into a variety of interesting adventures. That first summer back in California, while readjusting to my life, I felt inspired to complete a mini-triathlon in Sharon's honor. That involved swimming a half-mile, biking twelve miles, then running three miles. If my sister could undergo two brain surgeries, chemotherapy and radiation, not to mention facing the impending end of her life, then I could certainly sweat for a few hours.

This was not a logical goal; I am a slow runner, a mediocre swimmer and bicyclist. Not to mention that I'd just returned from eight months of strolling the streets of Aix eating *croissants* and *pain au chocolat*. But it felt right to take on the challenge.

My daughter Heather agreed to do the triathlon with me, and on the day of the event, a volunteer wrote our ages on our arms and legs with black markers, twenty-five and fifty-one, respectively. I looked around at the other women competing and felt a surge of fear in my stomach. These women were serious looking athletes, with rippling muscles and determined looking faces. What had I gotten us into? The scared voice whined. But it was too late to turn back.

Heather and I swam together and finished that first hurdle. Then she took off and I didn't see her again till she trotted back to meet me and encourage me in the last few yards of the run. We ran across the finish line holding hands, with Sharon cheering us on.

I've since completed four more mini-triathlons, always in Sharon's honor and to raise money for cancer research. I'm still quite average, but have even finished third in my age group a few times. Always the whiney voice complains; I have done it anyway. Sharon watched and cheered at two of them.

Royce and I rekindled our relationship and stayed together for about six months; he helped me through those challenging first months. It then became clear that we were first and foremost, very good friends and our time as a romantic couple came to an end. Shortly after that, he met his wife Mary and we all continue to enjoy a rich friendship.

My sister Sharon's health continued to decline and she needed my help more and more. She never lost her loving and kind ways, even near the end, when she could no longer walk or get out of bed.

It was a privilege to be close to her during her last days, to hold her hand and let her know that she was so loved and cherished. We lost her early on a February morning in 2003 and shivered in a freezing wind as we buried her a few days later. I have never forgotten her love and carry her memory close to my heart.

My mother died at age ninety-one, four years after my sister. She didn't change, but my own growth and centeredness allowed me to accept her and relate to her from a more peaceful place.

Gilbert passed away in 2008, but I was able to be there at his funeral and sit with the family in the front pew. It was clear that the love that began all those years before, between my father and Gilbert, lived on and had made such a difference in so many lives.

I visit Huguette each time I go to France and her grandson Romain's wife, Vanessa, shares photos of their adorable children and news on Facebook. I look forward to seeing them this year again.

As I've learned from living on my farm, no matter how bleak winter seems, my old apple trees burst into pink and white blossoms each spring. Those same flowers turn into crisp and delicious apples that we enjoy in the fall. After all those losses, in 2009, my life took a turn in an exciting new direction, a new spring, of sorts.

I thought of a man who I'd met thirty years before when he'd led a training that I'd taken. I'd never forgotten how dynamic he was and how much he had contributed to my life then, giving me the courage to take risks and to trust. Following a hunch, I found him on the Internet and contacted him to thank him.

A few months later we met to discuss his book, *Living Awake*. Right away, I knew that he was the partner I'd been waiting for. At first, however, he wasn't that interested in me.

But because I was willing to risk and trust, we navigated what seemed to many like a rocky start and now have a deep and powerful relationship, a true adventure and journey that I am grateful for each day.

Finding my partner fulfilled another dream that I had carried for over thirty years. We were married at the farm in 2012, outside on a sunny June day, surrounded by friends, family and adorable grandchildren.

When Maïté saw the wedding day photos, she wrote, *"tu respire de bonheur,"* you radiate happiness. And about my husband, Landon, *"il est beau comme un prince,"* he is as handsome as a prince. She said it well. I hope to take Landon to Aix and to receive my special monk's blessing on our marriage.

The farm and I continue to grow and change. Chickens now cluck and dig in the garden, sharing their delicious eggs. We enjoy lots of berries and organic veggies. The orchard still gives us apples, pears, peaches, plums and figs. The birds steal all the cherries and the squirrels the nuts, but I'm working on convincing them to share more with us. The grandchildren love helping to gather the eggs, climbing up into the tree house and soaring through the air on the swing on the giant oak tree.

My husband has supported my desire to be a writer, even building me a sunny writing studio near the garden. As I write this, I'm looking outside at the blue sky, white puffy clouds and the spreading branches of an old walnut tree. The chickens happily dig for worms after a spring rain.

Even after sixteen years, each day when I plan my day, I still write the same three words at the top of the page, *croyez-en-soi.* Believe in yourself. Those words take me back to that chilly evening in Paris when I saw them in the store window and they nourished and sustained me. They still do.

Since my marriage in 2012, I have written three memoirs. The first, *Falling in Love Backwards, an Unlikely Tale of Happily Ever After,* co-authored with my husband, Landon Carter, tells our love story. The second, *Reunion, La Réunion, Finding Gilbert,* tells the story of my father and Gilbert and the power that love story has had over my life. And now, this book is the third. I find writing to be a challenging adventure that continues to stretch me beyond my limits, yet fulfills me in a deep and powerful way.

Achieving my long-held, cherished goal of living in France

gave me the courage to know that dreams can come true at any age. I believe that wishes carried for years are full of magic and infused with the energy of that earlier age. We all could use a dose of magic, and fulfilling a long held goal can provide that.

The only thing that matters is that, as Willa Cather said so well, it meets *"our original want; the desire which formed in us in early youth, undirected and of its own accord."*

Those desires are the most powerful because they hold an element of mystery within them. They're not logical and can't be explained, but they call to us and refuse to stop.

I believe that great inner riches wait to be discovered in the depths of those yearnings. Like a grand treasure hunt, the clues can only be found by following that other path that takes us out of our normal, everyday life.

And so my wish for you is that you allow yourself to fulfill your desire, whatever it is, while there is still time to enjoy it and that you do it with all your heart.

Oh, and one last thing. Be sure to have the time of your life!

Wishing you all the best,
Diane Covington-Carter

June, 2016

Acknowledgements

A deep thank you to my 'first readers' Marilee Ford, Cheryl Murray, Dee Robinson and Heather Williams. And to Sands Hall, editor extraordinaire, for her patience and commitment to helping me to polish the prose. Margaret Campbell is a whiz at layout, cover and all things technical, and we are so grateful to have her help in our projects.

Bente Carter provided wonderful advice on cover design, and Genevieve Crouzet and Maïté Le Dantec helped me with the French words and phrases. Pilar Guzmán, editor in chief at *Condé Nast Traveler*, allowed me to use her words for my last chapter, and Louis B. Jones, writer, for my first chapter.

Ashley Olson, Executive Director of the Willa Cather Foundation, generously gave permission for the use of quotations from the works of Willa Cather. A special thanks to Phil Cousineau, author of *The Art of Pilgrimage: The Seeker's Guide to Making Travel Sacred*, who allowed a variety of quotations from his book.

And always, a huge thank you to my husband, Landon Carter, who provides me with the love, support, and encouragement to risk and trust, live life to the fullest, and to complete my writing projects.

Author's Note

For readers who have read my memoir *Reunion, La Réunion, Finding Gilbert*, you will notice some overlap in the two stories. The scene when I first heard French, *croyez-en-soi*, those first few days in Paris and finding my apartment in Aix are a few examples. These details played such an important role in both stories, so please forgive the repetition.

About the Author

Diane Covington-Carter graduated with honors from UCLA where she studied French and Cultural Anthropology. She has received awards for her writing, photography, and NPR commentaries. In 2013, she co-wrote *Falling in Love Backwards, an Unlikely Tale of Happily Ever After*, with her husband, Landon Carter. In 2014, she completed her memoir, *Reunion, La Réunion, Finding Gilbert*.

She lives with her husband on an organic apple farm in Northern California and off the grid near the beach in Golden Bay New Zealand. This is her third memoir. For more information go to www.DianeCovingtonCarter.com.

CPSIA information can be obtained at www.ICGtesting.com
Printed in the USA
BVOW06s1913140716

455619BV00013B/145/P